CHASING
AMERICAN
MONSTERS

About the Author

Jason Offutt grew up on a farm near the town of Orrick, Missouri. In his life, he's been a farmhand, journalist, photographer, bartender, and the mayor of a small town.

Jason's books include the novels *Bad Day for the Apocalypse*, its sequel *Bad Day for a Road Trip*, and *A Funeral Story*; the collection of short horror *Road Closed*; the parody survival guide *How to Kill Monsters Using Common Household Objects*; the humorous travelogue *Through a Corn-Swept Land: An epic beer run through the Upper Midwest*; and the paranormal titles *Haunted Missouri*, *What Lurks Beyond*, *Darkness Walks: The Shadow People Among Us*, and *Paranormal Missouri*. Jason also writes a weekly syndicated humor column.

He lives with his family in northwest Missouri where he teaches college journalism and keeps humanity safe from the inevitable invading Martian space army.

CHASING
AMERICAN
MONSTERS

251 CREATURES, CRYPTIDS, AND HAIRY BEASTS

MAINE GOATMAN

OZARK HOWLER

WASHINGTON BIGFOOT

JASON OFFUTT

Llewellyn Publications
Woodbury, Minnesota

FIRST EDITION
Eighth Printing, 2023

Book design by Samantha Penn
Cover design by Kevin R. Brown
Cover illustrations by Michael Koelsch / Shannon Associates, LLC
Editing by Holly Vanderhaar
Interior illustrations by Ty Derk

Llewellyn Publications is a registered trademark of Llewellyn Worldwide Ltd.

Library of Congress Cataloging-in-Publication Data
Names: Offutt, Jason, author
Title: Chasing American monsters : over 250 creatures, cryptids, and hairy
  beasts / Jason Offutt.
Description: First edition. | Woodbury, MN : Llewellyn Publications, 2019. |
  Includes bibliographical references and index.
Identifiers: LCCN 2018053960 (print) | LCCN 2018059921 (ebook) | ISBN
  9780738760063 (ebook) | ISBN 9780738759951 (alk. paper)
Subjects: LCSH: Monsters—United States. | Animals—Folklore. | Animals—
  United States—Folklore.
Classification: LCC QL89 (ebook) | LCC QL89 .O35 2019 (print) | DDC
  001.944—dc23
LC record available at https://lccn.loc.gov/2018053960

Llewellyn Publications
A Division of Llewellyn Worldwide Ltd.
2143 Wooddale Drive
Woodbury, MN 55125.2989
www.llewellyn.com

Printed in the United States of America

Other Books by Jason Offutt

Acknowledgments

Writing a book is an arduous process. It is highlighted, of course, by the exciting research and writing portion where the author sits in front of a computer with a cup of coffee and cries.

I'm joking. We only cry sometimes.

There are people who make the process easier. In my case, it's my family that (occasionally) gives me the time to sit in front of my computer without a toddler in my lap. I can't say the same about the family cat. Gary, you're a detriment to the creative process. There. I said it.

I'd like to thank the wonderful people I've worked with at Llewellyn Worldwide, Amy Glaser and Holly Vanderhaar, without whom you wouldn't be reading these words.

I'd like to thank Ben Grundy and Aaron Wright at Mysterious Universe who gave me the forum to share my original monster stories. Check out all the great content at mysteriousuniverse.org. Seriously. And don't forget to listen to the MU podcast. It's amazing.

And lastly, a shout-out to podcaster Tim Binnall, who not only has been gracious enough have me appear on his show *Binnall of America Audio* multiple times, he once challenged me to use his name in all my books, hence making him a permanent fixture in the Offuttverse. Here's mention number one, Tim. You're welcome.

For my mother, who suffered silently through a young Jason Offutt's monster fascination. I never outgrew it, Mom. Sorry about the Bigfoot thing.

CONTENTS

FOREWORD

WHEN JASON OFFUTT ASKED me if I would be interested in writing the foreword for his new book, I immediately said "Yes!" I have followed Jason's work for more than a few years and it has always proved to be captivating and intriguing—and written in an entertaining and atmospheric style. Jason's new book is no different. So, with that said, what will you discover in the pages of *Chasing American Monsters*? A more accurate question might be: what *won't* you discover? I'll tell you: not much!

Jason's new book is packed with tales that range from the creepy to the spine-tingling, and from the bizarre to the amazing. Of course, it helps when the writer has a flair for keeping his audience entranced, which is exactly what Jason does. In less capable hands, a state-by-state study of the monsters of America might come across as tedious and repetitive—and quickly, too. Fortunately, you can dispel all such thoughts from your mind.

From page one onward, *Chasing American Monsters* is guaranteed to grab you (by the claws and jaws, of course). As for the contents, what we have here is a book that addresses matters relative to the field of cryptozoology (the study of unknown animals, such as Bigfoot and the Yeti), the domain of the supernatural, and the world of monster-hunting—and blends them all into a fascinating story of incredible proportions.

Tales of rampaging werewolves comfortably sit next to wild accounts of long-necked lake monsters. Stories of living, mighty mammoths; of ferocious, winged humanoids; of creepy, evil gnomes; and of savage Wildmen of the woods, will make you ponder on just how much we know (or *don't* know) about the United States and what *really* lurks in its forests, rivers, lakes, woods, and caves.

It would be somewhat of a cliché to say that Jason's book should best be read on the proverbial dark and stormy night, when the wind howls, the rain pours, the lightning flashes, and that old, tall tree in your backyard creaks and groans alarmingly. Hey, sometimes a cliché works perfectly.

Monstrously entertaining!

—Nick Redfern
Nick Redfern is the author
of many books, including
Paranormal Parasites and *Shapeshifters*.

ꟼNTRODUCTION

HUMANITY HAS ALWAYS HAD monsters: creatures that lurk in our periphery, skulking, stalking, waiting until we're at our most vulnerable to show themselves. In the early days of humanity, sometime between climbing out of the trees and creating stone tools, there were real monsters. The cave bear, the woolly rhinoceros, the cave lion, the moa—all capable of instilling fear in man because they were all capable of killing us.

Humanity lost many of its real monsters during the late Quaternary megafaunal extinctions (around 11.7 thousand years ago); however, the rise of civilization brought us new monsters, like the minotaur, the cyclops, griffins, and dragons—all attempts to explain nature and theology with humanity's growing intellect. As we've found throughout history, as society changes, so does its monsters.

Many of the creatures in *Chasing American Monsters* may sound familiar. When people move to a new land, they bring with them more than just their families, their heirlooms, and their traditions. They bring with them their legends and, in some cases, the things that have always lurked in their shadows and hidden under their beds. The Banshee of the South Dakota Badlands has Irish roots, stories of the Tommyknockers of the mines in Pennsylvania and California came across the pond with settlers from Cornwall, and Connecticut's Black Dog of Hanging Hills sounds suspiciously like a British hellhound. Native American legends are scattered throughout this book, as are beasts never heard of before.

Legends of the European werewolf began in ancient Greece; however, these shape-shifting creatures started to appear in earnest across Europe in the medieval times because real wolves were a serious problem. Also at that time, people who didn't fit into the mold cast by the powerful Roman Catholic Church must be in league with the devil, so humanity created witches.

As technology changed, so did the creatures that terrified us. Mary Shelley's *Frankenstein* (published in 1818) was a direct result of scientists of that age (such as Italian physician Luigi Galvani) experimenting on the dead with newly-harnessed electricity. Victorian-age authors (1837 to 1901) terrified their audiences with more monsters like Shelley's—monsters that were once human, like Count Dracula, the Mummy, Dr. Jekyll and Mr. Hyde, and the Invisible Man. Decades later, the movie versions of these monsters reignited our fear in such creatures to reflect the horror of the Great Depression and both World Wars.

Once humans took to the air, our monsters changed again— they came from the sky. From H.G. Wells's Martians in *The War of the Worlds* (1898), to *Predator* (1987), to *The Avengers* (2012), our modern scientific monsters come from outer space. And starting with *Godzilla* (1954), the horrors of a nuclear world were quite evident on our movie screens.

Humans need monsters. They help us deal with the real horrors in life, mainly our fear of the unknown. According to the book *The Monster Show: A Cultural History of Horror* by David J. Skal, monsters help us "process our fears" about reality in a way that makes them less immediate. If a person is afraid of the artificial intelligence Skynet in the Terminator movies, they may not look too closely at the Amazon Echo in their own kitchen.

Today's popular monsters, vampires, Bigfoot, lake creatures, dogmen, and Black-Eyed Kids have their own place in our lives. In our modern world of science, there seem to be few places on our planet left to explore, fewer mysteries to solve. So, when someone sees a hairy, eight-foot-tall apelike man walking through their yard, it makes legends real, it brings the unknown into our homes and makes the impossible seem all too possible.

I fell in love with monsters a long time ago. I can even pinpoint the month—July 1971. That's when Joan Mills and Mary Ryan encountered a hair-covered, seven-foot-tall, three-toed, apelike monster near Louisiana, Missouri. I won't go into detail here; there's more about this monster later. I read stories about the creature for weeks that summer in *The Kansas City Star* (sure, I was a kid, but already a newspaper nerd) and I was hooked. Here was a monster—a Bigfoot named Momo—in my home state. I spent a lot of time outside that summer searching for giant footprints, wandering the cornfields surrounding my house hoping to have a run-in with the monster, and listening to my mom yell at me for trying to find it.

I never found the monster Momo (the sightings were 207 miles away, after all), but that didn't quell my interest. There were unknown creatures in this world—the Abominable Snowman, the Loch Ness Monster, dragons, living dinosaurs, extraterrestrials, lizard men, gnomes—and I wanted to know about them. All of them. I still do.

I'm not alone.

According to an Angus Reid Public Opinion poll, 29 percent of Americans believe Bigfoot is real, and 24 percent of Scots are as convinced of the existence of the Loch Ness Monster. A *60 Minutes/Vanity Fair* poll showed 30 percent of Americans believe in extraterrestrials and 33 percent believe in ghosts. A Gallup poll showed 18.8 percent of the American public is convinced Bigfoot and the Loch Ness Monster will eventually be discovered.

There are people out there, traipsing around forests and searching the depths of the world's lakes searching for these beasts. They are cryptozoologists (from the Greek *kryptos*, which means "hidden," and *zoion*, which means "animal"). Although usually not taken seriously by science, cryptozoologists do have an important job because at one point, all animals were unknown.

European scientists didn't see a living okapi until 1901, a mountain gorilla until 1902, a giant panda until 1916, a Congo peacock until 1936, and a megamouth shark until 1976. There are between fifteen thousand and eighteen thousand new species (half of them insects) identified every year. However, the most famous cryptid find is the coelacanth. According to science at the time, this six-and-a-half-foot-long saltwater fish became extinct about sixty-six million years ago. But on December 22, 1938, Captain Hendrick Goosen called South African museum curator Marjorie Eileen Doris Courtenay-Latimer (that name's a mouthful) to come look at a strange fish he'd caught. She went to Goosen and couldn't believe what she saw—the fish was a coelacanth. Take that, science.

If all these once unknown creatures exist, why couldn't something like Bigfoot? You know, a possible remnant Gigantopithecus, a possible remnant Neanderthal, a possible unknown species of North American ape. Whatever Bigfoot is, I think it just may be out there. I have faith in you, big guy.

I hope you enjoy *Chasing American Monsters*. Each chapter explores a state and brings you a view of unique beasts that lurk in its darkness. So, let's go. Be sure to bring along a flashlight, some snacks, maybe a jacket, pepper spray, and a nice canvas bag for the ever-sad, continuously weeping Squonk. Oh, and some good running shoes wouldn't hurt. You know, for all the other monsters out there that want to eat you.

CHAPTER 1
ALABAMA

ALABAMA, IN THE SOUTHEASTERN United States, is known as the Heart of Dixie. Although it ranks near the middle of the states in both size and population, Alabama does boast one of the largest inland waterway systems in the country at fifteen hundred miles. The state is mostly covered in plains, although the northern part of Alabama is filled with mountains. The state has four national forests, the largest natural rock bridge east of the Rocky Mountains at 148 feet (the largest west of the Rockies is the Landscape Arch in Utah at 290 feet), and a five-mile-wide crater made when dinosaurs still roamed the earth. The first electric trolley system in the world was unveiled in Montgomery in 1886, but it wasn't until the 1950s that the story of Alabama changed. In 1950, German scientists, including Wernher von Braun, were brought to the Redstone Arsenal in Huntsville to develop rockets, which in turn started the American space program. On December 1, 1955, Rosa Parks, an African American woman, refused to give her bus seat to a white man in this

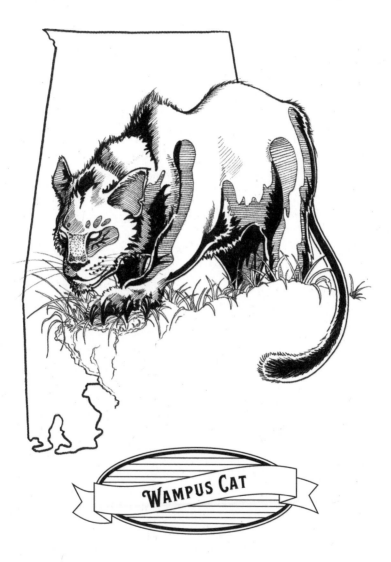

WAMPUS CAT

segregated state. This act became a symbol of the civil rights movement. Famous people from Alabama include Helen Keller, Olympic gold medalist Jesse Owens, baseball hall of famer Hank Aaron, author Harper Lee, and former Secretary of State Condoleezza Rice.

And then there are monsters.

The White Thang

Reports of the White Thang (yes, "Thang") date back to the 1930s, and reports of the monster vary. It has been described as everything from a dog to a Bigfoot to a ghost; but two things are constant—the monster's long white hair and its scream.

In the book *Legends and Lore of Birmingham and Central Alabama* by Beverly Crider, George Norris, an eyewitness in the 1940s, saw the monster, and "it looked like a lion...you know, bushy, betwixt a dog and a lion. It was white and slick with long hair. It had a slick tail, down on the end of the tail a big ol' bush of hair."

In the 1930s, the monster was said to run on all fours—even climbing trees to wait for people to walk beneath it. In later decades, it has been described as upright and at least seven feet tall, although witnesses say they can't make out any detail of the monster, like hands or facial features.

But it's not the beast's appearance or behavior that causes fright (people who've encountered the White Thang say it's nonthreatening); the monster's scream is what shatter's people's spirits. The shriek, like a woman or a baby crying, not only barks in the woods at night, witnesses have heard the sound come from the hulking, white-haired monster as it loomed over them and screeched into their face.

The Wampus Cat

When residents of Trussville began to discover their pet cats and small dogs slaughtered by an animal in 2014, official thoughts went to coyotes, but according to the Mobile *Press-Register*, canines didn't match eyewitness reports. One unnamed witness told the newspaper, "Several of the residents have confirmed it is a feline creature. It jumps tall fences and is extremely quick."

Thoughts of Trussville citizens went to one cause—the Wampus Cat.

This spectral panther–sized beast has been reported across the American Southeast for centuries. Although there are numerous legends about the origin of this cat, the following two are most common in Alabama.

The first legend comes from a Native American tradition. A Cherokee woman, suspicious of her husband's hunting trips, dressed in the skin of a mountain lion and followed the hunting party into the woods. She came upon the hunters sitting around a fire listening to stories about magic. She hid, staying to hear these stories that were forbidden to women. The men discovered her, and cursed her to spend eternity as a half-woman, half–mountain lion.

The second legend is slightly more modern, but just as magical, or at least Wellsian. According to the *McDowell News* of Marion, North Carolina, during World War II, the United States military succeeded in crossbreeding mountain lions and gray wolves in rural Alabama in an attempt to create a species of intelligent, vicious creatures to use as messengers in a war zone.

A few males and females of this new species escaped the military compound, and began to breed in the wild, becoming known as the Wampus Cat.

Or maybe the Wampus Cat is just a mountain lion, although Kevin Dodd from the Alabama Department of Conservation and Natural Resources denies any such animal exists in the state.

"There aren't any giant cats in Alabama," Dodd told the press.

The Alabama Metal Man

The woman on the other end of the telephone call was frantic. Falkville police chief Jeff Greenhaw answered the telephone shortly before 10:00 p.m. on the night of October 17, 1973, and heard the excited voice of a resident of rural Falkville claim a spaceship had landed just outside town in a field. The chief grabbed his camera and left the police station, arriving at the sight of the landing at precisely 10:00 p.m.

There was no ship in the field. There was, however, a monster.

Greenhaw encountered a bipedal creature wrapped in metal —and it advanced on him, according to an article written by B.J. Booth for NICAP (National Investigations Committee on Aerial Phenomena, a UFO research group). "It looked like his head and neck were kind of made together," Greenhaw told reporters. "He was real bright, something like rubbing mercury on nickel, but just as smooth as glass."

When Greenhaw trained his police cruiser headlights on it, the creature bolted across the field. Greenhaw pushed the car to thirty-five miles per hour across the bumpy terrain, but the monster quickly outdistanced it.

"He was running faster than any human I ever saw," Greenhaw reported.

Although the metal monster was never seen again, neither was the ship. The entity could still be wandering northern Alabama.

CHAPTER 2
ALASKA

ALASKA IS BIG. AT 663,300 square miles, it's about the size of Germany, Poland, and France combined. To put its size into perspective, if Alaska were a sovereign nation, it would be the eighteenth-largest country on the planet. This picturesque state is filled with scenic (if cold) ocean views, thick forests, the highest mountains in the United States, one hundred thousand glaciers, and abundant wildlife. The one thing it's not filled with is people; Alaska's population is 737,259—comparable to Detroit—and half of them live in the Anchorage metropolitan area. That works out to a population density of just 1.2 people per square mile. Alaska also has 6,640 miles of coastline, which is more than all the other states combined. That's a lot of open area for bears, moose, and killer whales, but it's also a haven for monsters.

WOOLLY MAMMOTH

Living Mammoths

From the Pliocene era (five million years ago) to the early Holocene (11,700 BCE until now), various species of mammoths lumbered across North America, Europe, Asia, and Africa. Although science agrees the species went extinct about ten thousand years ago, one pocket of woolly mammoths was still alive on Russia's Wrangel Island until 1650 BCE The pyramids at Giza were already one thousand years old at that point. Chew on that for a while.

However, a smattering of reports claim the eleven-foot-tall, six-ton animals have lived into modern times. Footage in Russia shot by a Nazi photographer during WWII appears to show a woolly mammoth walking through the snow. Native Americans in Canada have stories of these tusked beasts living in the northern wilderness. There's also this case published in the November 28, 1896, edition of the *Portland (Maine) Press* of Col. C.F. Fowler who heard of woolly mammoths in Alaska.

According to the article, Fowler was in Alaska to purchase ancient mammoth ivory from the local Inuit people when he noticed blood and rotting flesh on the roots of some tusks. When Fowler asked an elder where the tribe got the tusks, the elder told him that "less than three months before a party of his young men had encountered a drove of monsters about fifty miles above where he was then encamped, and had succeeded in killing two," Fowler wrote.

When Fowler spoke with the hunting party they described a creature from another age.

"Their ears were suddenly saluted by a chorus of loud, shrill, trumpet-like calls, and an enormous creature came crashing toward them through the thicket, the ground fairly trembling beneath its ponderous footfalls," Fowler wrote. "They were armed with large caliber muskets and stood their ground, opening fire on the mammoth. A bullet must have penetrated the creature's brain, for it staggered forward and fell dead."

In the article Fowler also said Alfred P. Swineford, second governor of Alaska, claimed there were "large herds of these monsters" above Snake River and Alaska's Seward Peninsula.

If these giants of the past still live, Alaska would be the place. Nice weather for it.

Iliamna Lake Monster

In a sparsely populated area of southwest Alaska (with 109 residents in the entire region in 2010) lies the 1,012-square-mile Iliamna Lake, home to Chinook salmon, lake trout, northern pike, and Ilie, the Iliamna Lake Monster. The lake itself, at seventy-seven miles long, twenty-two miles wide, and 988 feet deep, is the largest lake in Alaska, and capable of hiding the thirty-foot-long, square-headed beast.

The monster, known as Gonakadet by the native Tlingit people, was viewed as a god with the body of an orca and the head of a wolf; it was known to eat fishing boats. Early Russian explorers reportedly saw the creature at Iliamna Lake, and sightings have continued to this day. Modern reports come from explorers and biologists who have seen the thirty-foot monster, sometimes described as aluminum colored, other times as black with a white stripe. One report has an airplane snagging the beast with a tuna hook; the monster towed the plane around the lake before those aboard could release the cable.

There were multiple sightings in June 2017 near the town of Kakhonak. A number of people on June 19 and in the ensuing days saw something large emerge from the lake, according to radio station KDLG in nearby Dillingham.

"There was more than one, at least three," local resident Gary Nielson told the station. "The first was the biggest, maybe double the size of a thirty-two-foot gillnetter. The animal either blew like a whale, or spit water from his mouth or something. The smaller animals behind him did the same but not as dramatic. They were black or very dark gray … I am at a total loss as to what they could be."

Experts have claimed the Iliamna Lake Monster is everything from a white sturgeon, to a sleeper shark, to a beluga whale, all of which can reach a length of about twenty feet and have access to the lake, but the locals know better. Iliamna Lake is home to a monster.

Kodiak Dinosaur

Kodiak Island lies just 176 miles from Iliamna Lake, and is the scene of another sighting of a water monster. The shrimp boat *Mylark*, equipped with state-of-the-art sonar equipment, spotted something in the waters off Kodiak that the people aboard could only describe as a dinosaur.

The boat coasted past the island in 1969 attempting to map the sea floor when the equipment detected an object swimming about 330 feet below the *Mylark*—the object was two hundred feet long. The largest living sea creature, the blue whale, only reaches one hundred feet in length, and doesn't fit the description of what the crew of the *Mylark* saw that day—a creature with two pairs of flippers, a long, slender tail, and a long, thin neck topped with a small square head.

The crew told the *Kodiak Mirror* they thought they'd seen a dinosaur.

Giant Birds

In 2002, scores of Alaskans told the *Anchorage Daily News* they'd seen gigantic birds overhead. Villagers from Togiak and Manokotak in southwestern Alaska reported seeing the bird, which was "much bigger than anything they have seen before." Moses Coupchiak, forty-three, was working on his tractor when he saw the bird, and couldn't believe it. "At first I thought it was one of those old-time Otter planes," he said. "Instead of continuing toward me, it banked to the left, and that's when I noticed it wasn't a plane." (Otter planes are single-engine, propeller-driven aircraft that can be fitted with floats to take off and land on water, or skis to take off and land on snow. They were often used for search and rescue.)

John Bouker, a pilot and the owner of Bristol Bay Air Service, was skeptical of the reports of giant birds until he saw one himself. While flying near Manokotak he looked out his window and, "there's this big…bird," he told the *Daily News*. "He's really, really big. You wouldn't want to have your children out."

Raptor specialist Phil Schemf said there's nothing the size of that bird alive anymore. "I'm certainly not aware of anything with a fourteen-foot wingspan that's been alive for the last hundred thousand years," he said.

That we know of.

Steller's Sea Ape

German zoologist and botanist Georg Wilhelm Steller saw something in the mid-1700s that still has historians scratching their heads—a sea ape.

Steller was the naturalist aboard the *St. Peter* from 1741 to 1742 during the Great Northern Expedition to map a water route from Russia to North America. The expedition was wrought with conflict, scurvy, and a storm that wrecked the *St. Peter* on Bering Island. It is called Bering Island because the expedition leader Vitus Bering hadn't succumbed to scurvy at the time of the crash. He soon did.

While on the island, Steller identified several unknown animals, such as Steller's sea cow (a now-extinct species of dugong), Steller's eider, Steller's sea eagle, and Steller's sea lion.

But on August 10, 1741, while anchored off Shumagin Island, Steller categorized a creature never seen before or since.

While observing the waters off the shore, Steller claimed to have seen a five-foot-long animal in the water that defied science. It was covered in gray fur with a red belly, a head like a pig with whiskers, pointed ears and large eyes, and a shark's tail. The creature took notice of the boat and began to show off by playing with a bit of seaweed until Steller attempted to shoot it, but missed. The sea ape disappeared under the water and from popular knowledge.

There are many logical explanations for Steller's sighting, but the most telling piece that makes the sea ape's existence doubtful is that Steller omitted it from his official report.

Were-otter

The Kooshdakhaa, or "Land Otter People," of southeastern Alaska have terrorized the Tlingit people for centuries. Like the Gonakadet wasn't enough to worry about. According to *Alpinist Magazine*, the Kooshdakhaa are a race of people who can shape-shift into otters, but not before ensnaring humans in a web of cuteness (otters are adorable), and turning the humans into Kooshdakhaa themselves. Kooshdakhaa often assume the form of a human's loved ones to ease the deception. Once a human be-comes a Kooshdakhaa, his position in the afterlife is forfeit—the soul is trapped upon earth.

But the Kooshdakhaa are a finicky folk, prone to Kooshda-khaa transformation one minute and acts of kindness the next (such as rescuing drowning sailors), or simply shredding a vic-tim's flesh and spilling his entrails. You know, just because.

The Tlingit kept dogs to protect against the Kooshdakhaa. Not only could the dogs identify a Kooshdakhaa (whether be-cause of their nature or the fact that Kooshdakhaa may be car-rying pot is uncertain), but the Land Otter People are afraid of dogs. They're also apparently afraid of copper, fire, and urine.

Actor Charlie Sheen told the celebrity news website TMZ in 2013 that he traveled to Alaska with friends to search for the Land Otter People. However, his expedition came back empty-handed. "It obviously knew our group was far too skilled to be snowed in this fashion so it stayed hidden like a sissy," Sheen told the website.

Were-otters are also apparently afraid of Charlie Sheen.

CHAPTER 3
ARIZONA

THE LAST OF THE contiguous states to join the Union (on Valentine's Day, 1912), Arizona is known for its deserts, high heat, and the mile-deep Grand Canyon, which is one of the Seven Wonders of the Natural World. But Arizona isn't just desert and canyons; the northern part of the state is filled with mountains, ski resorts, forests, and creepy-crawlies. Famous people from Arizona include Apache leaders Cochise and Geronimo, labor leader Cesar Chavez, politician Barry Goldwater, Wonder Woman actress Lynda Carter, and singer Linda Ronstadt.

Mogollon Monster

The Mogollon Rim is an almost two-thousand-foot escarpment that runs through the central part of Arizona. Covered in Ponderosa pine forests, it's the perfect hiding place for the Mogollon Monster.

DRAGON

As first reported in the *Arizona Republican* in 1903, I.W. Stevens encountered the bipedal Mogollon Monster close to the Grand Canyon; it was drinking the blood of mountain lions. This human-looking creature with long white hair and beard that "reached to his knees," sported two-inch claws on its fingers. When the monster noticed Stevens it threatened him with a club.

Throughout the years the Mogollon Monster has been described as black, gray, or white, square headed or round, but all reports are of a tall hair-covered being on two legs with a humanlike hairless face. Although many people have equated the monster to Bigfoot, one hiker claims the monster is a troll. When hiking the Mogollon Rim Canyon Point Sinkhole Trail, the hiker saw the creature on its knees drinking water from a pool making "noises like a pig." The "troll" had long bluish-gray hair and a humanlike face "full of bumps." When it saw her, the troll stood on two legs and ran away. This sounds much more like the club-wielding bloodsucker from 1903 than a Bigfoot.

Dragons

Farther south is Tombstone, a 1800s boomtown that was the location of the famous Gunfight at the O.K. Corral—a shoot-out between the Clanton Gang on one side and the lawmen Wyatt, Virgil, and Morgan Earp, and Doc Holliday, on the other. Tombstone was also once known for a dragon.

According to *Mysteries and Miracles of Arizona* by Jack Kutz, two cowboys rode into Tombstone on June 7, 1890, with the skin of a what they claimed to be a "giant flying lizard" they'd killed outside town. The cowboys chased the beast on horseback before shooting and killing it. The dragon measured ninety-two feet long with an eighty-foot wingspan, an eight-foot-long head, and eyes "the size of dinner plates," the cowboys claimed. The battle was captured in the April 26, 1890, *Tombstone Epitaph* newspaper.

Werewolves

Werewolves, in various forms, have existed in many cultures across the world. From the medieval European werewolf that dominates horror movies, to Native American skinwalkers, the image of a man changing into a beast has terrified people for centuries. Sitting safely in a cozy house, watching television, the werewolf stalking the night is nothing but legend. But for a group of teenagers in Tempe, that idea is dead wrong.

From a 2009 Interview

The glow of city lights bathed the Arizona night in gray as four teenagers walked onto the Shalimar Golf Course in Tempe. Earl, now an adult, was in high school when he and his friends grew bored with their weekly Bible study meeting and walked outside, onto the course.

"My girlfriend says something like, 'Hey something just jumped out of that palm tree,'" Earl said.

The trees were approximately thirty-five feet tall, so the other teens laughed and resumed their conversation. "A few seconds later she lets out a bloodcurdling scream, just pure shocked terror," Earl said.

As Earl turned toward his girlfriend, he saw something he couldn't believe. "I look in the direction and there's a . . . creature lumbering along the wall toward us," Earl said. "It was as tall as me, six foot, hunched over, huge snout like a werewolf."

The beast, blacker than the night surrounding it, lunged toward the teens and they ran. "It was chasing after us," Earl said. "It was running along the wall toward me and I just turned and ran, I didn't think to look back."

The teens never saw the thing again, although something about the encounter still confuses Earl. "It was in the middle of town," he said. "That's what always gets me about that thing. Not out in the woods or at a secluded cabin, but in Tempe, Arizona."

Giants

Gigantic human remains, sometimes with red hair, have been reported across America, many of them in the desert Southwest. A giant human skull was once found in a cliff dwelling south of Winslow, Arizona, according to *The Complete Guide to Mysterious Beings*, by the great paranormal investigator John Keel. "It was so big that a size 7[E] Stetson was placed on it and 'looked like one of those tiny hats merrymakers wear on New Year's.'" The skull also had a gold tooth.

Workers reportedly discovered a huge stone coffin in Fort Crittenden in 1891. The coffin held a skeleton that measured twelve feet tall, and had twelve toes.

A man named Samuel Hubbard is said to have found the mummified bodies of two giant humans (fifteen to eighteen feet tall) in a cave in the Grand Canyon in 1923. This is fourteen years after the *Phoenix Gazette* published the account of explorer G.E. Kinkaid, who said he discovered a cave in the canyon filled with Egyptian artifacts, including mummies.

CHAPTER 4
ARKANSAS

THE STATE OF ARKANSAS in the southern US is known for its lush green mountains, roaring rivers, and University of Arkansas football. It's home to the headquarters of the world's number-one retailer, Wal-Mart, and is the birthplace of musician Johnny Cash and former US president Bill Clinton. It's most famous monster is the Fouke Monster, a Sasquatch-type creature immortalized in the 1972 movie *The Legend of Boggy Creek*.

Fouke Monster

The late 1960s and early 1970s were awash with Sasquatch sightings in the United States. A rash of famous occurrences were reported to the press between 1971 and 1974 in Fouke County, although earlier sightings go back to the 1940s.

Starting in 1946, people around Jonesville, a tiny village near the town of Fouke, began seeing a seven-foot-tall, three-hundred-pound gorilla-like creature wandering the woods. Residents called it the "Jonesville Monster." It wasn't until 1971,

OZARK HOWLER

when locals around Boggy Creek in Fouke County spoke with a reporter for the *Texarkana Gazette*, that the creature became known as the Fouke Monster.

The 1971 reports began on May 2 when Elizabeth Ford, sleeping on the couch in her home, was attacked by what she thought was a bear reaching toward her through a nearby screen window. When she screamed, her husband Bobby and his brother Don burst outside and chased the creature away. However, what they saw wasn't a bear. The Fords watched as a tall, lumbering creature with the gait of an ape disappeared into the trees. The thing left something behind: a smell like a combination of a wet dog and a skunk. When the Fords investigated the next morning, they found seventeen-inch-long three-toed footprints in their yard.

The monster didn't leave the Fords alone; it terrorized them. It frequented their rural home, leaving claw marks on the porch and damaging the siding. The Fords fired numerous shots at the beast, but they never knew if they hit it.

The Fords weren't alone. Later in May, motorists encountered a large ape crossing US 71 in front of their car. A few months later three-toed footprints were found all over the county, including in a soybean field owned by a gas station owner who reported them to the game warden. The warden had no idea what to make of the tracks.

After the story hit the national news, people flocked to Fouke County to hunt the creature. The Little Rock, Arkansas, radio station KAAY offered $1,090 for anyone who bagged the monster. Three years later, with still no creature body in hand, the sightings stopped.

The Fouke Monster was made into a pop culture phenomenon in 1972 with the release of Charles B. Pierce's documentary-style motion picture about the sightings entitled *The Legend of Boggy Creek*. Although sightings of the beast had slowed to a trickle by 1974, in 1978 people started finding large three-toed footprints in the area again, and they haven't stopped. A steady stream of reports has continued, the latest being a May 2017 sighting near Fouke when a man and woman saw a tall, hairy humanoid figure standing in the trees near Boggy Creek.

Attention apparently hasn't waned either. In 2017, a journalist sent a Freedom of Information Act request to Fouke Mayor Terry Purvis to release any information the city had on the creature.

"I am literally speechless," Purvis told the *Texarkana Gazette*. "The kicker is, by law I have to answer this. I will do my best and try to be professional in my response. I don't have anything for them. The Fouke Monster and Southern Sasquatch never visited downtown."

Ozark Howler

The Ozark Mountains in north central Arkansas are covered in pine trees, hickory, and several species of oak. A number of endangered species live in these forests, and so does the Ozark Howler.

The Howler has been reported to be a great cat, or dog, or bearlike beast with eyes that glow red from behind a black pelt. The monster stands four feet tall at the shoulder, and some witnesses say the beast has horns, according to Fayetteville and Fort Smith's 40/29 News. But the one aspect every witness agrees upon is the Ozark Howler's piercing, terrifying cry, described as everything from the bugling of a bull elk, to the laughter of a hyena (more on that later).

Many people have dismissed the Ozark Howler as a hoax, but Howler sightings stretch back to the early 1800s. A number of residents of Red Oak reported seeing the Howler in 1846; so did residents in nearby Branson, Missouri, in 1998, and in Jasper, Arkansas, in 2011. Is the Howler a hoax? Witnesses don't think so.

Gowrow

This twenty-foot-long lizard with jutting tusks reportedly lurks in dark, dank caverns in northern Arkansas. The earliest report of the Gowrow was in the January 31, 1897, edition of the *Arkansas Gazette*; it describes a man's claim that he killed one of the monsters near Marshall, and sent the remains to the Smithsonian Institution, although there are no records of it. The man, William Miller of Little Rock, gathered a group of hunters to track down the beast that had been feasting off local livestock. They tracked the Gowrow to its lair, where it charged them, shaking the ground and felling trees before they shot it to death. Other reports of Gowrow encounters scatter northern Arkansas.

Hyenas

The hyena of North America, Chasmaporthetes, lived during the Plio-Pleistocene era, 4.9 million to 780,000 years ago. It was lean limbed and sprinted like a cheetah. Have a smattering of American hyenas survived until this modern age? Some residents of Arkansas think so. According to a post at arkansashunting. net, a hunter in Izard County claims a man saw a hyena cross the road in front of him. He didn't believe the man until others came forward reporting to have seen the same animal.

Similar stories are posted on the topix.com website. A woman says she was scouting deer with her ex-husband "years ago" on Lost Mountain in northern Arkansas, when they saw a strange animal with a band of coyotes. "Running with this pack I noticed an animal that wasn't anything like them," the woman wrote. "It had a large hump on its back, legs were sorta low to the ground, and the color was way off. I'd seen them on Discovery Channel enough to know what it was so I started freaking out screaming, 'Oh my God, it's an honest to God hyena.'"

White River Monster

Named Whitey for its home in the White River, this gray-skinned river monster first appeared in 1915. A local plantation owner who saw Whitey said it looked about "as wide as a car and three cars long," according to an article in the *Christian County Headliner News*. The White River, which is twenty-six feet deep at flood stage, doesn't seem deep enough to be the home of a monster that large. But reports of Whitey continue.

Witnesses saw a twenty-foot-long gray monster with a horn and a spiny back in the river in 1971. Investigators discovered fourteen-inch, three-toed tracks of a large animal that apparently emerged from the river, and walked on the shore, crushing brush, and breaking small trees. Hundreds of people have claimed to see Whitey over the years.

In 1973, the Arkansas State Legislature designated a stretch of the river the White River Monster Refuge and made it illegal to harm the monster there.

Pterosaur

According to science, these flying reptiles lived from the late Triassic period to the end of the Cretaceous period, which would mean the creature has been extinct for at least sixty-six million years. However, people have reported seeing these winged monsters all over the world, including in Arkansas.

A group of people saw a large flying creature near Texarkana in 1982. The creature was featherless, and had a pointed beak and a head crest. When they got home they looked up the monster in a book; it was a pterosaur.

According to the *Christian County Headliner News,* a woman named Laura Dean was driving to the grocery store when a large creature with gray, leathery skin and a head crest appeared from beneath a bridge and flew within six feet of her car. The wings were bat-like, with claws at the tips, and the tail was tipped with a diamond-shaped flap. What terrified her was the size of the beast. It was larger than the Chevrolet S-10 pickup she drove.

CHAPTER 5
CALIFORNIA

HUMANS HAVE LIVED IN California for at least fifteen thousand years. In 1848, the United States acquired the area that would one day become the state of California for fifteen million dollars after signing the Treaty of Guadalupe Hidalgo, which ended the Mexican-American War. California, famous for Hollywood, the Golden Gate Bridge, and earthquakes, is the most populous state in the union, and the third largest in area after Alaska and Texas. Outside the large cities (16.37 million people in the greater Los Angeles area) lie great expanses of desert, mountains (including Vasquez Rocks Natural Area Park, where Captain James T. Kirk battled the Gorn in *Star Trek*), and forests. Despite the number of people, there's plenty of room in California for unknown creatures, like Patty.

BILLIWHACK MONSTER

Patty

When it comes to Bigfoot sightings, this is the granddaddy of them all. Or, more accurately, grandmamma.

On October 20, 1967, cowboy Roger Patterson and his friend Bob Gimlin were riding quarter horses near Bluff Creek, nearly twenty-five miles from the nearest town, Orleans. The men were looking for something legendary and, although they knew it was a Bigfoot hotspot (numerous giant, manlike footprints had been found there in the late 1950s), they were a bit surprised when they found it.

Walking fewer than a hundred feet away from the men, along a creek bed amongst fallen trees and scrub left from a flood in 1964, was something tall and hairy. Just what the two men were looking for—a Bigfoot. The sight of the creature spooked their horses. Patterson, riding in front, slid off his mount, pulled a rented 16 millimeter film camera from his saddlebag, and began shooting.

The creature took notice of the men and their horses, but didn't seem to care. The large apelike beast, with obvious breasts, kept ambling up the creek bed, swinging its arms. Filming continuously, Patterson followed the female Sasquatch while Gimlin dismounted his horse and drew his rifle. The monster looked at the men briefly over its shoulder before walking into the woods.

Patterson shot a hundred feet of film, the last 23.85 of which were of the Bigfoot who became affectionately known as "Patty." The film is only 59.5 seconds long, but it is the first and best evidence that the legendary Bigfoot exists. Although many people believe the Patterson-Gimlin film to be a hoax, nothing definitive has ever been proven. Hollywood special effects experts at the time, like Bill Munns, examined the footage and said they couldn't replicate it. The footage may actually be of a Bigfoot.

The Canadian Broadcasting Corporation interviewed Gimlin on the fiftieth anniversary of the event (Patterson died of cancer in 1972) and he's still sticking by his story. When asked if he believes "to this day" he and Patterson saw a Bigfoot, Gimlin said, "Yes, absolutely. No question in my mind."

Dark Watchers

The coastal Santa Lucia Mountains run for 105 miles, from Monterey County to San Luis Obispo County. The western slopes of the mountains are covered with Ponderosa pine, Santa Lucia fir, and coastal redwood. The mountains are also home to the Dark Watchers.

The first peoples to speak of the Dark Watchers were the Chumash Indians, who once lived in the two-hundred-mile stretch between Malibu and Paso Robles. When European settlers first came to the region, they too saw these giant human silhouettes that stand on ridges, and seem to stare across the mountains. When watched themselves, the Dark Watchers fade from sight.

Legend has it that these humanoid creatures rarely appear to anyone who is carrying a gun, or is dressed in weatherproof clothing; they only reveal themselves to people who wander the mountains in more old-fashioned garb.

Nobel Prize–winning author and California native John Steinbeck wrote about the Dark Watchers in his short story "Flight," as did poet Robinson Jeffers in his poem "Such Counsels You Gave to Me."

Although people have seen the Dark Watchers looking across the Santa Lucia Mountains for hundreds of years, when approached these watchers vanish, leaving nothing behind, not even a footprint.

The Billiwhack Monster

A monster terrorized Santa Paula during World War II and the years shortly after. The creature, tall and apelike with horns like a ram, frequented the haunts around the Billiwhack dairy and ranch off Wheeler Canyon Road. The Billiwhack Monster had long gray hair, and was massively muscled. The beast was reported to throw large rocks at people and pound on the hoods of witnesses' cars, leaving dents, according to the book *Ghosts of Ventura County's Heritage Valley* by Evie Ybarra.

The monster was allegedly the result of the government's attempts to make a super soldier in an area lab, but it escaped. Although seen often throughout the 1950s and up until 1964, sightings of the Billiwhack Monster have grown few and quite far between.

The Black Demon

The prehistoric Megalodon shark was as long as a bowling lane, was as heavy as a Boeing 757, and was armed with six-inch-long, serrated, heart-shaped teeth designed to rip through bones and heavy cartilage. It was the largest predator to ever swim the seas, and did so from about 23.03 to 2.58 million years ago. Could the Megalodon still swim our world's oceans? Some eyewitnesses believe so.

A thirty-one-foot long shark was seen off the coast of New Zealand in 2014, according to the *New Zealand Herald* (for comparison, great white sharks can grow to up to seventeen feet long). One that "was huge. Like dinosaur huge," was spotted off Fish Hoek beach in Cape Town, South Africa, according to the *Guardian* newspaper. Naturalist David Stead reported seeing an "immense shark" in 1918, and in the 1960s, fishermen claimed that a shark longer than their fifty-five-foot fishing boat circled the vessel before swimming off.

Sailors off the coast of California have similar stories, but none is as persistent as the Black Demon from the Gulf of California. This shark is said to be more than sixty feet long. In 2008, a fisherman named Eric Mack said his boat was rocked by the Black Demon. Although he didn't see the entire beast, the tail fin rose five feet out of the water, according to *Discovery News*.

Evil Gnomes

When a woman named Tammy moved her family to a rural house near Porterville, she didn't know that something wicked waited for them. "We always got the feeling of being watched," she said.

One spot on the farm especially put her on edge: the barn. She soon discovered why.

"One evening my son … and I had just come back from grocery shopping," she said. "We parked and got out of the car and as I was opening up the back to get the groceries out I noticed a movement out of the corner of my right eye."

When she turned from the car, it happened again. "This time I heard a very freaky, very evil-sounding chuckle," she said. "I looked in the direction of the sound and there standing about fifty yards from my son and I was what I can only describe as a gnome."

The bearded creature was about two to three feet tall, and it wore a gold shirt and a red pointed hat. "That thing grinned at us and the creepy grin spread from ear to ear," she said.

She dropped the groceries, grabbed her son, and ran to the house, the wicked little man cackling after her. Tammy burst inside through the kitchen and slammed the door. As she tried to tell her daughters about her panic, something moved outside the kitchen window. She looked, and saw the top of the thing's red, pointed hat. It had to be about ten feet off the ground.

She never saw the gnome again, but until the day she moved, she would hear the gnome's chuckle come from the old barn.

Giant Cockroaches

The old motel sat like a row of army barracks on the side of a grassy hill in California City, about halfway between Bakersfield and Barstow. Peggy, who was from Texas, was traveling to Los Angeles from Las Vegas in the late 1990s when she stopped at the motel for the night—a night that burned itself into her memory. "I never went back there again, it was so horrendous," Peggy said.

The motel had a big cockroach problem.

Late in the evening, as Peggy sat inside her room watching VH1, someone knocked on the door. She approached the door and pulled it open as far as the chain would let her. She wasn't prepared for what was in the hall. "A human voice behind that door had asked if I could hand him some bed linen," she said. "I never saw his features, but in the slight crack of the door I could see a long upturned giant cockroach cleaning its legs frenetically."

When the creature, which Peggy marks at about six-and-a-half feet tall, saw her through the crack in the door, it spat something brown toward her. She screamed. "Why?" the creature asked, but Peggy didn't answer. She threw open the door to her room and ran down the hall, past a motel employee crumpled on the floor.

As Peggy neared the exit, the great cockroach thundering close behind, it grabbed her. "It was frightening," she said. "It grabbed onto my cotton dress and I couldn't get away from its doubled-barbed hands on my wrists." The thing's antenna brushed against Peggy's face, her vision grew cloudy and she thought she might faint. "Then I remembered a Chuck Norris movie and I dropped to my buns on the floor and kicked its ankles out from under it with my tennis shoes," Peggy said. "Then I kicked it in the face."

Peggy got up and ran, but felt the creature closing on her as she threw open the door at the end of the hallway and slammed it shut on one of the creature's antennae. "You never heard such a loud high-pitched scream come out of living matter as I did," she said. "You wouldn't believe how loud these giant upright walking cockroaches could shriek."

Then Peggy ran blindly into the night. A young man who had seen the giant cockroaches chasing Peggy called the police on a pay telephone next to the motel and seconds later two police cars screamed into view and the roaches disappeared over a hill.

"Bugs multiply real fast," Peggy said. "People I talked to said they'd seen things flitting behind trees... What if they're breeding?"

CHAPTER 6
COLORADO

COLORADO IS KNOWN FOR its Wild West history, 1858's Pike's Peak Gold Rush, great skiing and rafting, and three NFL championships. Colorado also boasts a variety of geography, such as high plains, most of the southern Rocky Mountains, and desert. Colorado, the eighth-largest state, was once home to actors Douglas Fairbanks, Lon Chaney, and Tim Allen; boxer Jack Dempsey; Barbie doll creator Ruth Handler; and Frank Welker (the voice of Fred from *Scooby-Doo*). Colorado claims seven of the ten tallest mountains in the contiguous United States, and produces a wealth of dinosaur fossils. Dinosaurs? Hmm. I wonder if any are still walking around.

Living Dinosaurs

Myrtle Snow, of Pagosa Springs in north central Colorado, told *Empire* magazine in 1982 that, as a child, she'd seen living dinosaurs. In 1935, when she was three, she saw "five baby dinosaurs." After the dinosaurs attacked a local farmer's sheep, the

43

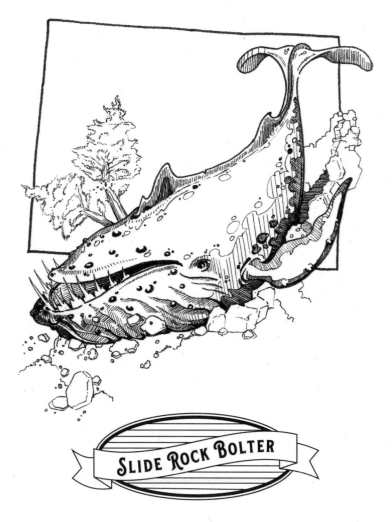

SLIDE ROCK BOLTER

farmer shot one, and she got a good look at it. "My grandfather took us to see it the next morning," she told *Empire*. "It was about seven feet tall, was gray, had a head like a snake, short front legs with claws that resembled chicken feet, large stout back legs, and a long tail."

A fanciful tale of a living theropod dinosaur, such as a velociraptor or a juvenile *Tyrannosaurus rex*? Maybe, if it was the only one.

Over the years, residents of Pueblo, in southeastern Colorado, have claimed to see theropod dinosaurs running through the countryside. The creature, described as a small T. rex at about three feet tall, has powerful hind legs, tiny front legs, and a long tail.

Slide Rock Bolter

Miners and lumberjacks in the 1800s came out of the mountains with tales of a land whale that lived on the slopes and fed off any animal that wandered in front of it—especially people. This huge creature would lurk at the tops of mountains, lying in wait for days, unmoving. It latched itself onto the mountainside with hooks on the end of its massive fluked tail. When prey approached, it would release the hooks, and slide down the slope, tearing through trees and boulders before swallowing its dinner with its huge, saw-toothed mouth.

One of the earliest printed accounts of the Slide Rock Bolter was in the 1910 book *Fearsome Creatures of the Lumberwoods* by William T. Cox. As the years went on, and Colorado became a vacation spot, the Slide Rock Bolter has been blamed for missing tourists it apparently loves to dine on.

Vampires

In 2010, a woman drove her SUV into a canal in Mesa County and told authorities the wreck was caused by a vampire, according to the *Denver Post*. She was driving on a dirt road near the town of Fruita on the Western Slope when she saw a vampire on the road. Terrified, the woman, not identified by police, put the SUV into reverse and drove it off the road, where it overturned. Authorities said she was not under the influence of drugs or alcohol.

This isn't the first report of a vampire in Colorado. In the late 1800s and early 1900s, the mining town of Lafayette, east of Boulder, attracted workers from the eastern United States, as well as Europe. One of these workers was Fodor Glava from Transylvania—the Lafayette Vampire.

When Glava died in 1918, rumors started circulating that he was an undead bloodsucker. When a tree sprouted from his grave on what would be the chest region of Glava (now six feet under), people were convinced the tree grew from a stake driven into his heart, as Claudia Lund, curator of the Lafayette Miner's Museum, told Colorado's News9. A blood-red bush that grows next to the grave didn't help matters.

CHAPTER 7
CONNECTICUT

ONE OF THE FIRST thirteen British colonies in North America, Connecticut revels in American patriotism, demonstrated by its nickname the "Constitution State." Heck, its state song is "Yankee Doodle." Famous people from Connecticut include American Revolution names like Ethan Allan, Benedict Arnold, and Nathan Hale; showman P.T. Barnum; abolitionist John Brown; inventors Samuel Colt (revolver), Charles Goodyear (vulcanized rubber), and Edwin H. Land (Polaroid); pediatrician and author Dr. Benjamin Spock; and Noah Webster, the dictionary guy. Although it's the third smallest of the United States by area (110 miles long and 70 miles wide), it's the fourth most densely populated, and, with 1.9 million acres of forestland, Connecticut can still hide plenty of unknown creatures. Like this doggie:

GLASTONBURY GLAWACKUS

The Black Dog of Hanging Hills

Just north of the downtown of Meriden in southern Connecticut are the Hanging Hills, which run through Hubbard Park, an 1,800-acre mountainous area on the National Register of Historic Places. Covered in a forest broken by cliffs and rocky outcroppings, this land is the romping place of the Black Dog.

The first reported sighting of the Black Dog by someone other than a local was in the late 1890s, when New York geologist W.H.C. Pynchon visited the Hanging Hills and discovered a medium-sized black dog followed him. The dog remained with Pynchon the entire day, neither barking nor whining, and when the scientist started to leave, the dog, which he was happy to have along on his day of hiking, vanished into thin air. He wrote about his encounter in the April–June 1898 *Connecticut Quarterly*.

Locals, he later discovered, knew of the Black Dog, and although its first and second visits were pleasant, the third sighting of the dog was anything but.

On a second trip three years later, Pynchon saw the dog again. A companion, however, had been to the area before, and for him this was the third encounter with the dog. Legend has it the third time seeing the Black Dog means a death knell. Pynchon's companion soon after fell off a cliff to his death. "If you meet the Black Dog once, it shall be for joy," Pynchon wrote in the *Connecticut Quarterly*. "If twice, it shall be for sorrow; and the third time shall bring death."

The Black Dog is similar to black spectral hounds in traditions across Europe, most specifically the British Isles. These demonic dogs, with names like the Black Shuck and Barghest, often foretell death.

Melon Heads

Something terrifying with a taste for human flesh lurks in backwater areas across Connecticut; something small—the Melon Heads. These small humanoids with huge heads, bulging eyes, and wiry limbs lurk in the woods, and prey upon passersby. Claimed to be everything from incestuous backwoods rednecks to descendants of Colonial witches, the Melon Heads live in the forest, and bite people who dare tread on their territory.

In Fairfield County, the Melon Heads are supposedly inbred cannibal offspring from around twenty insane asylum patients that escaped when a fire destroyed the asylum and killed the administration, staff, and most of the patients, according to a story in the *Torrington (Connecticut) Register-Citizen*.

Although more of an urban legend than actual monsters, the Melon Heads cause travelers on the lonely, tree-covered country roads in rural Connecticut to drive just a little bit faster.

Sea Monsters

Reports of sea monsters off the coast of Connecticut have existed since the early European colonization of New England. Most sightings were of long, snakelike creatures, some with bodies "as wide as a horse," with a "big black head as large as a flour barrel, and with eyes as big as small plates." The serpents were said to be forty to one hundred feet long. One sighting reported, in a 1881 article in the *New York Times*, that a huge serpent, green with black spots, swam by a yacht out for a pleasure cruise, and scared the bejesus out of the those on the boat.

But serpents aren't the only monsters seen off the Connecticut coast. In 1895, Captain Obadiah Donaldson wrote that his ship collided with an octopus just off the coast—an octopus more than sixty feet wide with tentacles stretching at least one hundred feet, according to the July 17, 1895, *Chicago Tribune*. Like a scene from Jules Verne's *Twenty Thousand Leagues Under the Sea*, the monster wrapped one of its tentacles around the ship and began to drag it down under the water. A sailor named Frank Taylor chopped through the monster's arm with a meat cleaver, and the beast sank beneath the waves once more.

Glastonbury Glawackus

During the unusually cold winter month of January 1939, the residents of Glastonbury had something to worry about besides the snow—the Glastonbury Glawackus. This howling beast terrorized the nights that winter. A furry monster the size of a large black dog with the face of a cat slaughtered small dogs, goats, and sheep, according to a story in *The Hartford Courant*.

Hunters combed the forests and hills with dogs; the dogs occasionally chased something unseen through the brush, but the Glawackus remained elusive. Some claimed it was a mountain lion escaped from a zoo, or a Canada lynx in the area, but William F. Bonvouloir, a hunter from Hartford, encountered the beast. He saw a "beautiful black creature about three feet long with a tail two feet long leap out of the scrubwood," according to the *Courant*. He shot at it twice with a twelve-gauge shotgun, but missed both times.

As evidence of a monster near Glastonbury dwindled by that next July, hunters killed a big, brown wild dog, and claimed the end of the Glawackus, although many residents of Glastonbury had their doubts.

CHAPTER 8
DELAWARE

DELAWARE IS KNOWN AS "The First State" because it was the first state to ratify the United States Constitution. Delaware sits on the Delmarva Peninsula, and is bordered by New Jersey, Maryland, and Pennsylvania. The state gets its name from Virginia's first colonial governor, Thomas West, Third Baron De La Warr. Famous people from Delaware include actress Valerie Bertinelli; surgeon Henry Heimlich, inventor of the Heimlich maneuver; and two signers of the Declaration of Independence, George Read and Caesar Rodney. The second-smallest state in the Union, Delaware is one of the least populous, but it does have a few hairy critters.

Selbyville Swamp Monster

Two raccoon hunters trudging through the Great Cypress Swamp of Selbyville one night in the 1920s found something unexpected. The hunters were in what locals call "Burnt Swamp" because of a devastating fire in the 1930s. They knew

SELBYVILLE SWAMP MONSTER

something was wrong when their dogs froze and tucked tail, but they didn't expect what they encountered next. "They heard something screaming, and this horrible noise started coming toward them," author Andy Nunez told the newspaper *Coastal Point*. "Rather than fire on whatever it was, they backed away. Something large and heavy continued to follow them, snapping through the branches as it came."

The hunters had encountered the Selbyville Swamp Monster, a large, hairy, hulking beast.

Ralph Grapperhaus, an editor of the *Delmarva News*, claimed he created the Selbyville Swamp Monster as a hoax in the 1960s; he had dressed friend Fred Stevens in a hairy costume. Stevens used to terrify motorists on Route 54, and Grapperhaus printed stories of Swamp Monster hunts in the *Delmarva News*. Stevens revealed his part in the hoax in 1987. He'd stopped dressing as the monster after a few months, as hunts for the creature became common, and he feared for his life.

However, Stevens's claims don't account for encounters in the early part of the 1900s.

Mhuwe

This giant stalks the icy fields of winter in search of prey. Akin to the better-known Wendigo, the Mhuwe is a large, hairy beast that feasts on human flesh. According to a Delaware Indian legend, the Mhuwe are human beings who have become cannibals, and turned into monsters. One legend has a tribe taking in a Mhuwe, feeding it fruits, vegetables, and cooked animal meat until the monster transformed back into a man, according to the Native American website native-languages.org.

Zwaanendael Merman

Lying in a glass case in the Zwaanendael Museum in Lewes is a merman. The foot-long mummified creature arrived in Lewes in the 1800s, a present to the Lewes family from a sea captain. The merman has a fish's tail, humanlike arms, and a screaming humanoid head topped with white hair.

A thing of local legend, the Zwaanendael Merman is likely a hoax. The Division of Historical and Cultural Affairs in Delaware said the merman was "created in mid-nineteenth-century China using a shrunken monkey head, fish, hair, ivory, glass, oak, stain, varnish, and dye," according to an article in the Wilmington *News Journal*.

Or is it? A sea captain wouldn't lie, would he?

Bigfoot

For a long time, Delaware and Hawaii were the only two states in the Union without reported Bigfoot sightings. Delaware can't say that anymore. Three encounters, all in Sussex County in the southeastern part of the state, have been reported to the Bigfoot Field Research Organization in the recent years.

A college student at Delaware Technical Community College in Georgetown was driving home on a back road from a night class in January 2004 when he saw something he didn't believe existed. As he pulled up to a stop sign, the student noticed a figure standing next to a utility pole, staring out into a patch of forest. Thinking it was a man, he turned off his high beams and kept driving. As he approached the figure, he noticed its immense size, about eight feet tall, and the thing was covered in thick black hair. When the figure turned its crested head to look at the car, it casually turned back toward the woods as if the car didn't matter. Terrified, the driver sped away as quickly as possible.

A woman returning from a vacation with her family in August 2010 saw the head and shoulders of a Bigfoot standing over the corn in a field. No one else saw the creature.

A couple that had just returned home from the grocery store in November 2012 heard a tremendous scream followed by a series of knocks of wood on wood from a patch of trees behind their house. The sun had set about an hour before; the couple saw nothing, but was convinced a Bigfoot was near their house.

Bigfoot in Delaware? Could be.

CHAPTER 9
FLORIDA

ZOMBIES, CANNIBALS, AND CURIOSITIES. Florida is known for terrifying creatures that stalk the streets and swamps of this southern state, and that's just the locals, such as Jonathon "The Impaler" Sharkey of Tampa. Sharkey has run for the highest political office in the United States three times since 2004 in a bid to become the first vampire president, according to *CBS News*. He claims he's a direct descendant of Vlad the Impaler. He's also been accused of brainwashing teenage girls, and intimidating a judge. Just another happy, carefree story from the Sunshine State.

Even without the politicians, Florida is a scary place filled with alligators, hybrid man-eating pythons, escaped kangaroos, and herpes-infected monkeys.

Yes, herpes-infected monkeys.

But that's nothing compared to the Skunk Ape.

ST. AUGUSTINE MONSTER

Myakka Skunk Ape

An odd sort of Bigfoot, the skunk ape is said to resemble an orangutan more than the gorilla-like Sasquatch reported around North America. The skunk ape, named for the foul scent that accompanies it—"like a wet dog and a skunk, mixed together," according to *Smithsonian Magazine*—was seen often in Florida swampland throughout the 1960s and 1970s, and although sightings have declined since then, some of the most interesting encounters have been during the past twenty years.

In 2000, an unnamed woman sent the Sarasota County Sheriff's Department photographs of what she thought was an orangutan in her back yard. The beast had appeared on three consecutive nights at her house near the Myakka River, eating apples from her back porch. It smelled awful.

In 2013, Floridian Mike Falconer took a 1:55 minute video on his iPhone in the Myakka River State Park of a creature he claims to have been the skunk ape. The video of the distant, black, hairy creature is on YouTube.

Although Florida wildlife officials deny the existence of the skunk ape, the sightings continue.

Lake Clinch Monster

Lake Clinch in Polk County has a long history of a monster in its depths. In the 1928 book *A History of Polk County*, M.F. Hetherington documents tales of a huge creature in the lake. "The Indians many years ago insisted there was an immense serpent in this lake," Hetherington wrote. "In 1907 residents of Frostproof declared they had seen the monster, and that it must be thirty feet long."

Although called a serpent, the descriptions of the monster—with a humped back, long neck, and flippers—sound more like a plesiosaur.

The Polk County newspaper, the *Ledger*, refers to a passage in the book *My Pioneer Days in Florida*, 1876–1898, by Emily Bell, that claimed the beast was "green and black and a yellowish mingled colors" that was at least thirty feet long.

Muck Monster

Want a Muck Monster T-shirt? Well, monster aficionados can get a Muck Monster T-shirt, and a barbecue apron as well, in West Palm Beach, or they can just go to lagoonkeepers.org.

This monster, a large serpentlike creature, has been seen for years in Lake Worth Lagoon; however, it gained notoriety when two members of the nonprofit Lagoon Keepers organization, Greg Reynolds and Dan Serrano, took a boat out to fish a large log from the water. The log moved. The two followed it, but every time they closed to within ten feet of the "log," it submerged. This caused the two to say this obviously living creature was hiding in the muck. The duo shot video of the monster and sent it to a local television station, and Muck Monster mania was born.

Although there have been serious attempts by legitimate scientists and weekend cryptozoologists to investigate the creature, the crass commercialism of the area has turned the story of the Muck Monster into Muck Monster specials at local restaurants. The T-shirts and barbecue aprons are legitimate, and go to fund the Lagoon Keepers' efforts to keep the waterways clean.

Sauropod Dinosaur

Although the sightings had tapered off by 1975, between 1955 and 1961, the St. Johns River was hot with reports of a river monster. The reports weren't confined to the locals. Visitors, commercial fishermen, authorities, and seemingly everyone saw this creature—a huge, humped beast, with a long tail, long neck, and doglike head. A man from Lake County claimed he saw a dragon-like monster leave the water and eat plants from the banks, leaving crushed vegetation and broken trees in its wake as it moved through the brush, according to the book *Weird Florida: Your Travel Guide to Florida's Local Legends and Best Kept Secrets*, by Charlie Carlson.

St. Augustine Monster

In 1896, beachgoers at St. Augustine found something hideous on the sand—a corpse. The unidentifiable mess of a creature, quickly called the St. Augustine Monster, was an eighteen-by-ten-foot blob that smelled worse than the Skunk Ape. Scientists declared this beast, most probably from the deepest depths of the ocean, to be a giant octopus or squid. You know, a Kraken. This is the first verified occurrence of a "globster," an "unidentified organic mass" that washes up on the seashore, according to Smithsonian Institution Archives.

Although modern analyses of the monster (1995) show it may be the remains of a sperm whale, no one knows for sure what the St. Augustine Monster was. It may be Cthulhu.

CHAPTER 10
GEORGIA

GEORGIA, NAMED AFTER KING George II of England, is one of the original thirteen colonies. It was the birthplace of civil rights leader Dr. Martin Luther King Jr., singer Ray Charles, *Gone with the Wind* author Margaret Mitchell, and wrestler Hulk Hogan. Yes, THE Hulk Hogan. Of the thirty-seven million acres of land in Georgia, 24.8 million acres of that is forestland. The Peach State is the fourth-largest state east of the Mississippi River, and is home to mountains, rivers, and critters like the Altamaha-ha.

Altamaha-ha

The Altamaha River stretches 137 miles through the center of the state until it empties into the Atlantic Ocean near Brunswick. It pours the third-largest amount of fresh water into the Atlantic from the United States. It's also home to a beast known as the Altamaha-ha.

HOGZILLA

Looking like a cross between a sturgeon, a crocodile, and a seal, this thirty-foot-long monster is often seen near the city of Darien by fishermen and swimmers (why would you swim in a river with a monster?). Darien was founded in 1736 by people who have their own stories of a water monster: Scotsmen from Inverness.

Although part of the local Indian legend, the Altamaha-ha gained national notice in 1981 when a newspaper publisher saw the beast while fishing. He reported it as two humps, five feet apart, that were moving as fast as a speedboat. After that, other stories of monster sightings began hitting the press, such as a 1970s tale of a twenty-foot-long creature with the head of a snake, and another of an underwater creature that caused boats to bob in its wake. But these sightings were not the first. Where the Altamaha River dumps into the ocean, a sea captain saw a seventy-foot-long creature, "its circumference about that of a sugar hogshead," according to the April 18, 1830, *Savannah Georgian* newspaper. The creature held its alligator-like head eight feet out of water before it sank back into the depths.

Emily Burt, the Georgia Werewolf

The story of Georgia's werewolf began with a death.

When six-year-old Emily Isabelle Burt's father, Joel Hurt Burt, died in 1847, he left behind three other children—Sarah, Alpheus Joel, and Mildred Owen—his wife Mildred, and a tremendous amount of money. Wanting her children to have the best education possible, Mildred sent them to boarding school in Europe. When the children returned home to Pleasant Hill, near Talbotton, after a semester abroad, something was wrong with Emily, according to findagrave.com.

Emily, always shy and reserved, was even more so. She appeared to always be sick and she often complained of lack of sleep. Concerned with her daughter's health, Mildred began watching Emily closer. The girl would fall asleep, and then, when in a deep slumber, would rise and leave the house, walking into the nearby woods. Mildred asked her daughter about this, but Emily remembered nothing of her late-night journeys.

Gradually, as legend has it, her appearance changed. Her teeth grew to points and she began to sprout hair in odd places. People started to suspect that there was something seriously wrong with the girl, especially when local farmers began to see mounting evidence a wolf had been slaughtering their livestock (red wolves were once common in Georgia). The farmers attempted to hunt down the beast, but never found it.

Driven to a frenzy, the farmers eventually began to suspect the animal mutilations were caused by a werewolf. They awaited the next full moon and went out looking for the beast. They weren't disappointed. The party came upon a man-sized wolf that walked on two legs. They shot and hit it. The beast yelped and ran into the trees.

When Mildred heard shots fired in the night, she ran to Emily's room, but her daughter wasn't there. Terrified, the mother dashed into the woods and found her daughter lying in the dirt, bleeding. Emily had been shot. The local doctor arrived and saved Emily, but word soon spread of the little girl's injury on the same night the farmers shot the beast. People began to suspect she was a werewolf.

After the girl healed enough to travel, Mildred sent her back to Europe where, hopefully, she would be cured of lycanthropy.

Apparently, she was. In Emily's absence, the animal mutilations stopped and they did not start again when she returned. Emily, who became a successful businesswoman, lived to be seventy years old.

Hogzilla

The legend started in 2004 when hunting guide Chris Griffin said he shot a wild hog in the Georgia woods. He claimed the beast was twelve feet long, and weighed more than a thousand pounds. He shot it, lifted the body with a backhoe, a buddy snapped a picture, and the internet went wild.

"All sorts of thoughts were running through my head, and I was thinking, 'I'm gonna take a shot at this animal,'" Griffin told *ABC News*.

Labeled a hoax by many, *National Geographic* enlisted a "pig geneticist, a wildlife ecologist, and a pig behavior specialist" to test the animal. Hogzilla was real, although not one thousand pounds. The wild boar/domesticated pig hybrid weighed eight hundred pounds.

Hogzilla left the world—especially the small town of Alapaha, where the beast was shot—with two things to consider: (1) Where did Hogzilla come from? *National Geographic* couldn't figure out that one. (2) Are there more out there? Although not a thousand pounds, eight hundred pounds is still awfully big for a dangerous monster roaming the nearby woods.

Beavershark

This three-foot-long creature is a local legend of Pine Mountain. Sometimes reported to have the head of a beaver and the body of a shark, and other times to have the head of a shark and the body of a beaver, the beavershark swims in the lakes of Callaway

Gardens, preferring deeper water where it feeds on fish and turtles, although it is occasionally seen near shore to take bites out of swimming children, according to an article in the *Lake Destination Lanier* magazine.

Used as a warning to youth at local summer camps, the beavershark makes most of its appearances in places where souvenirs are sold.

The Wog

A boggy pond near Winder, called the Nodoroc by the local Creek Indians, is a mud volcano that once seethed and bubbled, emitting smoke, giving the brown bog a hellish appearance. This was fitting, seeing as Nodoroc is a Creek word that means "gateway to hell." The Creek Indians of the 1800s had built a stone altar at the bog, where they executed prisoners and tossed the bodies into the bog to suffer there for eternity. Legends state the Nodoroc is inhabited by the Wog.

The Wog is a demon dog about the size of a small horse, with long black fur, and longer front legs than hind legs. According to *The Early History of Jackson County Georgia*, by historian G.J.N. Wilson in 1914, "This gave him something of the appearance of a huge dog sitting on its tail." The monster has a long tail with a puff of white hair at the tip. The Wog, with its bearlike head, has blazing red eyes and a forked tongue that sticks out at least eight inches from its tusked mouth.

Although the Wog lurked in the Nodoroc and swept the dead under the churning mud with its tail, in the 1800s European settlers reported seeing the creature slinking around cabins, and frightening domesticated animals to death.

I'd say it would.

CHAPTER 11
HAWAII

HAWAII IS, WELL, IT'S Hawaii. A series of islands in the central Pacific with more gorgeous beaches, cliffs, waterfalls, volcanoes, and girls in bikinis than it knows what to do with. Apart from its geography and lush tropical vegetation, Hawaii is famous for its love of Spam, the late singer Don Ho, the lei, and the luau. Europeans discovered the islands on January 18, 1778, when English explorer Captain James Cook landed on one of the sandy beaches. Islanders killed Cook on Valentine's Day the next year for being a jerk (attempting to kidnap the king will get you that short-lived reputation). Shark attacks occur on Hawaiian shores, although in 2014, only three out of eight million visitors were attacked by sharks. Hawaiians have more to fear from Axis deer wandering into the roadway than from shark bites. Although Hawaii is the one state in the Union that has no reports of Bigfoot, there are still plenty of creepy-crawly monsters to go around.

Mo'o

Menehune

The little people of Hawaii, the Menehune, were builders. Gifted with great strength and architectural skill, these two-foot-tall creatures built works in stone, including dams, roads, and sacred worship sites known as *heiau*. The Menehune only appear at night, when they build their stone structures, passing stones from one to another in a long line. However, they only build when no one else is around. If their work is interrupted, they disappear.

One thing you don't want to do is anger them, like Lisa, Brian, and Noah, who went out one night on Kauai and experienced something that terrifies them to this day.

Under a clear moonlit sky, the three drove to an isolated beach on the south shore of Kauai, where they began to notice something wasn't right. "It is very dark at this place, as there are no major cities around," Lisa said. "We lit a fire." Then the horror began.

"I noticed that the rocks and roots and trees around us looked liked gnarled, grotesque faces," Lisa said. "I pointed it out to my two companions who agreed. I wasn't scared because I thought they were merely hallucinations."

As Noah built a fire, Lisa and Brian walked down a footpath through the tall grass and started seeing the shadows of small people. Frightened, Lisa and Brian hurried back to the fire. "We were right next to a heiau—a pre-contact place of worship for Hawaiians, like an altar," Lisa said. "I was very miffed that he would bring us to such a creepy and spiritually charged place."

Growing paranoid that they had upset something ancient by their presence, Lisa and Brian decided to walk to the heiau and offer the only food they brought with them—a pear—as a gift.

As they approached the heiau, Lisa couldn't go any closer and stopped. "The vibe of the place seemed very charged, not like when we had first arrived," she said. "We said a prayer out loud, stating our respect and that we were giving a food offering. Brian walked into the grass to deposit the pear and disappeared."

A few moments later, Brian came running out of the grass. It was full of little people who attempted to encircle him. They abandoned the fire and drove screaming into the night.

Pterodactyl

A twelve-year-old boy saw something near Honolulu in the early 1970s that shouldn't exist: a living dinosaur.

A creature with a wingspan of about thirty feet glided overhead. It had brown, featherless, lizard-like skin, and what he described as a horn on the back of its head. The boy didn't know if the thing had a tail; he was concentrating on the wings and head. The flying reptile slid slowly through the sky until it began to flap its wings, and disappeared over the horizon. Similar sightings have been reported from the islands in 1999, 2012, and 2013.

Mu

Vampires appear in various cultures across the world, and Hawaii isn't immune to their blood-sucking powers.

These three-foot-tall, naked monsters with toothless mouths that stretch across their faces live in caves with openings underwater. The Mu venture from their daylight hiding places to lurk in the shallows, and wait for victims. When the Mu attack, they drag their prey under the water into the caves where they suck on the victims until the blood is drained.

Mo'o

Nestled deep in Hawaiian legend are the Mo'o, Hawaii's dragons. The Mo'o are black lizards from twelve to thirty feet long.
They live in water—pools, springs and fishponds—and can shape
shift from a gecko to a dragon to a beautiful, seductive woman.

According to legend, three Mo'o captured a man betrothed
to the Hawaiian volcano goddess Pele. Angered, Pele sent her
sister Hi'iaka to the Mo'o's underwater cave to rescue him.
Hi'iaka slayed one of the Mo'o and freed the man.

Mo'o (the Hawaiian word for lizard, which is used commonly for geckos) is considered a guardian lizard god that pro-
tects people and sacred areas near springs. However, the Mo'o
are capricious, so people can never tell what they're going to
do. Some have been known to push people into rivers to drown
them. Two ways to appease a Mo'o are to praise them, or to feed
them a drink made from the awa root, which gets them intoxicated and makes the Mo'o swim from side to side.

The Mo'o may be more than legend. Some locals still believe
in these water dragons and can point to fishponds where they
live, such as in the historic whaling village of Lahaina, the village
of La'ie, Kalepolepo Beach Park, and Wailua Valley. The Mo'o
are also credited with keeping freshwater springs running.

CHAPTER 12
IDAHO

THERE'S A SERIES OF maps that made the rounds on the internet showing the average Brit's knowledge of United States geography. Out of twenty-two participants, only four got Idaho correct, probably because they'd guessed. A man named Paul wrote over Montana, Wyoming, and Idaho, "No one knows these ones." Too bad, Paul. These states are amazing. The earliest known human habitation in Idaho dates back fourteen thousand years. Butch Cassidy and the Hole in the Wall Gang tore through Idaho in the 1800s, and author Ernest Hemingway committed suicide there in 1961 (not Idaho's fault). The geography is stunning. Majestic, snow-covered peaks of the Rocky Mountains overlook wide, sweeping, forest-covered valleys and lakes, if you like that sort of thing. It's called the "Gem State," because almost every known gem has been found there, and also the "Potato State" because, you know, they grow potatoes. The governor of Idaho (since January 2007) is named "Butch" Otter,

LIVING DINOSAUR

which in itself is awesome. Apart from its beauty and Butch Otterness, Idaho boasts its share of monsters—especially wet ones.

Bear Lake Monster

Bear Lake, the "Caribbean of the Rockies," is 109 square miles of clear, cold water that crosses the borders of Idaho and Utah. Surrounded by mountains (and golf courses), Bear Lake is a popular spot for fishing, jet skiing, and snow sports. Visitors can also swim, if they don't mind the creature that dwells beneath the surface of the lake.

Reports of the Bear Lake Monster first surfaced in an 1868 edition of the Salt Lake City, Utah, *Deseret News*, when the newspaper published numerous sightings of the monster by locals. The beast has been described as everything from an enormous alligator with blazing red eyes, to a walrus without tusks, to a dinosaur.

The last reported sighting was in 2002, when local businessman Brian Hirschi claimed he saw "these two humps in the water" near his boat, according to the *Deseret News*. The humps disappeared, but something lifted his boat, and he saw a giant serpent neck break the surface. The beast had dark green skin, topped by a toothy head with "beet-red eyes." The beast roared, and disappeared back into the 208-foot-deep lake.

Although the person who filed the original report in the 1800s later claimed he'd made up the story, that doesn't account for Native American sightings, Hirschi's, and others.

Sharlie

Another lake monster, Sharlie (or Slimy Slim) is said to inhabit the sparkling blue waters of Payette Lake, an eight-mile-long, two-and-a-half-mile-wide lake near the Oregon border. Native Americans spoke of an evil spirit swimming in its 392-foot depths.

The first modern(ish) sighting of the creature was reported in 1920, when people working on the lakeshore saw what they thought was a log in the water, until the log swam away. Groups of people saw the monster in 1944, and again in 1946, all describing it as a plesiosaur between thirty and forty feet long. The creature was seen dozens of times between 1946 and 2002.

Despite skepticism about the creature, according to a report on Boise, Idaho's KTVB, locals are convinced Sharlie exists.

Living Dinosaur

From the depths of Idaho lakes, to its mountains, reports of monster reptiles abound. One of these reports occurred a few days before December 17, 1909, when two men saw a "giant" lizard that crushed trees when it walked.

A 1909 article in the *Carbon County News* claimed Joseph Cliffe and Walt Glifford were hunting in the hills when they heard a sound from an unknown animal. Moments later, crashing through the trees was a giant lizard with a crest behind its head, and horns on its face. The ground shook beneath its feet. The men ran up the hill, and eventually stopped to look down. The monster, they said, was scaled, with "a row of bony spikes" along its back. The animal, they estimated, was more than eighty feet long. Cliffe shot at the creature with his hunting rifle, but only managed to anger it. The hunters ran back to town, and told their story. Groups of armed men ventured out in search of the monster, and some saw it fleetingly, but they never got close enough to get off a shot.

CHAPTER 13
ILLINOIS

THE STATE OF ILLINOIS is known for the city of Chicago, the second-tallest building in North America (Willis Tower at 1,451 feet), the city of Metropolis in the southern portion of the state (named the Home of Superman in January 1972), and some of the best pizza in the United States. It was the home of four presidents—Abraham Lincoln, Ulysses S. Grant, Ronald Reagan, and Barack Obama—although Reagan was the only president to be born and raised there. It's the fifth most populous state in the Union, and the twenty-fifth largest. And, with 4.4 million acres of forestland, there's plenty of room for beasties like the Enfield Monster.

The Enfield Monster
Henry McDaniel heard scratching on his front door around 9:30 p.m. on April 25, 1973. When he looked out his window he saw something on the front porch that would terrorize the small community of Enfield for years. "It had three legs on it, a short

ENFIELD MONSTER

body, two little short arms, and two pink eyes as big as flash-lights. It stood four-and-a-half feet tall and was grayish-colored," he told the local press.

McDaniel shot at the creature, hitting it once. The monster hissed at McDaniel, "like a wildcat," then jumped like a kanga-roo and moved fifty feet in three hops. When the local police ar-rived at the McDaniel house, they discovered doglike footprints with six toes.

McDaniel said he saw the monster again at 3:00 a.m. on May 6. "I saw something moving out on the railroad track and there it stood. I didn't shoot at it or anything. It started on down the railroad track. It wasn't in a hurry or anything," he told local radio station WWKI. The station's news director wandered the area around McDaniel's house, and claimed to see a creature that looked like an ape.

An extensive search failed to turn up the monster. "If they do find it, they will find more than one and they won't be from this planet, I can tell you that," McDaniel told the local press. Specu-lation as to the monster's identity ranged from that of an escaped kangaroo to an escaped ape to an extra-terrestrial.

Farm City Monster

Four Farm City teens camping on private land were sitting around their campfire on the night of July 9, 1970, when they heard something big moving in the grass at the edge of the fire-light. One of the boys hopped in their car and switched on the headlights to reveal a manlike beast covered in long, gray-white fur. When the lights struck it, the creature ran off, according to an article in the *Bloomington Pantagraph*. The boys said the mon-ster was at least six feet tall.

That wasn't the last of the monster. A few days later, two dozen people claimed to see "a pair of eyes glowing at them in the dark," according to the *Pantagraph*. The Sunday after that, three more people saw the hairy creature, and even more people had witnessed it by the next Tuesday. "I didn't think it was as tall as they said it was," witness Bob Tharp told the newspaper. "It looked to be maybe three or four feet high."

Although numerous people saw the Farm City Monster, the only casualty assigned to the beast was the heavy canvas tent at the boys' campsite, which something with claws had torn to shreds.

Cole Hollow Road Monster

The 1970s was a big decade for monsters in Illinois. In 1972, a creature the locals around Cole Hollow Road called Cohomo (short for Cole Hollow Monster) was seen numerous times south of Peoria. The monster was eight feet tall, covered in white fur, and had only three toes.

The monster encounters began after a family picnicking at Fondulac Park in East Peoria claimed to see unidentified lights sink behind trees, followed by a trail of smoke. That night more than two hundred calls to the East Peoria Police Department reported the monster, which smelled like sulfur.

Although twenty-one years later a local man claimed he'd fabricated the story as a prank, that doesn't account for continued monster sightings, including similar descriptions of a beast labeled the Murphysboro Mud Monster and Bull Valley Monster.

Flying Humanoids

Since April 2017, more than fifty people in Chicago have reported seeing a flying humanlike entity that is sometimes described as resembling a huge bat, and sometimes an owl. In most cases, it has fiery red eyes; its screech is ear-piercing.

According to the *Chicago Tribune*, the first encounter was on April 7 in Oz Park on the North Side. A woman was walking her dog when she saw a seven-foot-tall man standing in the park. The creature was black and sported enormous wings. When the entity became aware of the woman and her dog, it spread its wings and shot into the sky. The encounter made an impression upon the woman.

"I felt like this thing could see right through me, read me, it knew what I was thinking, like it could stare right into my very soul," the woman said in the *Tribune*. "It was the most terrified I have ever been in my life."

Another encounter occurred on April 30. A man and his son were fishing in the Little Calumet River when they saw a black bird the size of a man flying overhead. Another man saw a man-sized bat around the Adler Planetarium on June 23.

Most of the sightings occur at night, although some happen in daylight hours. Some see the entity flying, while others simply see it perched upon rooftops. These 2017 sightings are similar to those from the same area in 2011.

Flying humanoids aren't new.

A humanoid was seen—and recorded by three different people—flying over Sequoia Park in Los Angeles in 2015. But it's the reports from Mexico that lend the most credence. A flying humanoid appeared in 1992 over the Sun Pyramid during the equinox. One appeared flying between buildings in the Agricola Oriental neighborhood in Mexico City. A police officer claimed to have been attacked by a flying humanoid in Guadalupe, Mexico, in 2004.

Some people are comparing the 2017 winged humanoid sightings in Chicago to the late-1960s Mothman sightings in West Virginia. More on that later.

Tuttle Bottoms Monster

In 1963, in the swampy land north of Harrisburg, a young man with a rifle stopped Saline County sheriff James L. Thompson and told him he was hunting a monster. The creature was at least eight feet long, as tall as a pony, and had a nose like an anteater, according to the *Harrisburg Daily Register*.

More than fifty people have reported seeing the creature since 1963, but the Tuttle Bottoms Monster remains a mystery.

Murphysboro Mud Monster

The small town of Murphysboro, less than twenty miles from the southeastern border of Missouri, was visited by a creature in June 1973, a creature the townsfolk have yet to forget—the Big Muddy Monster.

On the night of June 25 that year, a couple was kissing in a car on 23rd Street near a boat dock in Riverside Park when a scream from the nearby woods pried them apart. When they looked, a beast with whitish hair mottled by mud stood in the trees. It was about seven feet tall, walked on two legs, and was headed toward the car. Frightened by the creature, they started the car and sped away, stopping at the Murphysboro Police Station to report the incident.

Police took the report of this big "gorilla" seriously because the terrified couple confessed to the reason they were at the park in the first place—they were having an affair.

"There was no advantage for them to come up and report this," retired Murphysboro police chief Ron Manwaring told the *Southern Illinoisan* in 2005. Manwaring was a patrolman with the department at the time of the sighting.

Officers responded to the scene and, although the monster was long gone, there were twelve-inch-long footprints three inches deep in the mud. The monster left the investigating officers with something else, however. It screamed at them from deep in the woods.

Another report came into the station the next evening. Teenagers on a porch in a subdivision saw a tall, white-haired, muddy creature looking at them from the tree line. Manwaring was on duty at the time and responded to the scene, finding only a black substance on brush that emitted an awful stench.

Although the 1973 reports gained national attention, they weren't the first stories of the creature near Murphysboro. A man gardening in the 1950s claimed to have seen the exact same creature.

CHAPTER 14

INDIANA

THE STATE OF INDIANA is best known for sports, like the Indianapolis 500 and Brickyard 400 motorsports races, the NFL's Indianapolis Colts, the NBA's Indiana Pacers, and college basketball. It's also home to farmland, rivers, lakes, and plains. It's the thirty-eighth-largest state with the sixteenth-greatest population. Indiana has had its share of famous residents, such as the King of Pop, Michael Jackson; comedian Red Skelton; basketball great Larry Bird; actor James Dean; and KFC founder Colonel Sanders. Van Camp's Pork and Beans were created in Indianapolis, as was the rapid-fire weapon the Gatling gun. Green also seems to be a popular color there.

The Green Clawed Beast

While swimming in the Ohio River near Evansville on August 21, 1955, an unseen "clawlike hand" grabbed Mrs. Darwin Johnson and pulled her beneath the water, according to a story from radio station WKDQ. Her friend, Mrs. Chris Lamble

BEAST OF BUSCO

(married women apparently didn't have their own first names in 1955), lay sunning herself on a nearby raft when she heard her friend yelp, and turned to see her being pulled under.

The hand released Johnson, who swam to the surface only to be grabbed and pulled under again. She kicked free and pulled herself onto the raft with the screaming Lamble. Later, when treated for multiple injuries from the attack, a green handprint was found on Johnson's leg. The stain lasted for days. The women never saw the monster, and no reports have surfaced since.

Mill Race Monster

Two groups of girls in Mill Race Park in Columbus on November 1, 1974, reported encountering a "green, hairy, and large" monster. The first report was at 3:00 p.m., the second at 11:00 p.m., according to the *Columbus Republic*. During the 11:00 p.m. encounter, the monster jumped on the victims' car and left "claw marks in the paint."

Days later, city dogcatcher Rick Duckworth claimed to have seen the creature, and described it to the newspaper as looking "like a person wrapped in blankets and wearing a mask."

The park became flooded with monster hunters, so much so that the city had to close the park from dusk to dawn, stationing police around the entrances to turn away thrill seekers.

Although the sightings stopped as quickly as they began, the legend of the creature has left its mark on Columbus.

The Beast of Busco

In 1898, farmer Oscar Fulk claimed to see an enormous snapping turtle in a lake on his farm near Churubusco. Dubbed "Oscar" by the locals, the giant turtle was only a story until two fishermen, Ora Blue and Charley Wilson, saw the creature in the lake in

1948, according to the *Columbus Republic*. They claimed the turtle weighed at least five hundred pounds. Gale Harris, who owned Fulk Lake, also saw the creature and said he was going to capture it. The legend had grown, and so apparently had the turtle. Reports had the shell being as big as the roof of a car.

Although Harris drained the lake, the turtle was never found. That doesn't stop Churubusco from hosting its Turtle Days festival every June.

Crawfordsville Monster

In 1891, two ice deliverymen in Crawfordsville saw a "horrible apparition" flying over them. Their claim was bolstered by the local Methodist minister and his wife, who told the *Crawfordsville Journal* they saw a monster "about eighteen feet long and eight feet wide" fly through the air. It appeared to the minister and his wife to resemble a white shroud with "propelling fins." They didn't spot a tail or a head, but heard it wheezing from an "invisible" mouth. "It flapped like a flag in the winds as it came on and frequently gave a great squirm as though suffering unutterable agony."

Monster Snakes

Indiana has more than its share of stories of enormous snakes. The most terrifying is from Benton County.

A ghoulish snake that inhabits a cemetery west of Oxford, and feeds off the corpses within, has been reported for years. The creature, "measuring fifteen feet in length, as large in circumference as a good-sized stovepipe, with eyes of fire, adorned with horns underneath fully ten inches long... has been seen by at least a dozen people," according to the *Lafayette Courier,* September 3, 1889. Reports state large holes were discovered that lead into graves.

Other claims of monster snakes dot Indiana, from the twenty-five- to thirty-five-foot-long reptile seen near Greensburg in the 1920s, to the thirty-foot-long snake of fire seen by farmer Mark Weston near Alexander in 1893.

Meshekenabek

The Potawatomi Indians near what is now Rochester stayed away from Lake Manitou because of its inhabitant, the Meshekenabek. According to the book *Recollections of the Early Settlements of the Wabash Valley* by Sandford C. Cox, "The Indians would not hunt upon its borders, nor fish in its waters for fear of incurring the anger of the evil spirit that made its home in this little woodland lake."

The Meshekenabek, a dark, thirty-foot-long, serpentlike monster with the head of a horse, was seen in that lake in 1827 by men building a corn mill. The local blacksmith saw the beast and added it had "large yellow spots."

The monster was seen again in 1838 by two men who claimed the monster was "sixty feet long, and looked like a huge snake," according to the *Logansport Telegraph*.

Although enormous fish have been caught in the lake, no one has ever captured the Meshekenabek.

Crosley Monster

Something terrifying lurks in Jennings County's 4,228-acre Crosley State Fish and Wildlife Area—a hairy, eight-foot-tall monster with hooves and yellow, glowing eyes. The creature supposedly hides in the trees and leaps upon unsuspecting victims from the hidden boughs of the pines.

The Crosley Monster first appeared in 1958 and has stalked the fear of residents ever since.

One of the more recent encounters occurred in 2006 when four teenagers—Clint Maschino, Corey Mullikin, Robbie Evans, and Terry Snyder—camped in the wildlife area and came within mere feet of the beast. At about 11:00 p.m., the boys heard branches snapping as someone—or something—approached them through the woods. The teens thought it might be a deer until they saw its eyes, which were large, yellow, and glowing. The eyes were at least seven feet off the ground.

"I saw his shadow from our lantern and it was huge," Snyder told the *North Vernon Plain Dealer Sun*. "You could see from the shadow he had a bunch of hair, too. He looked filthy."

Not wanting to wait for the creature to act first, the boys took off running. The monster gave chase.

"He ran through the cornfield next to Grayford Road as we ran down the road. I could hear him knocking down cornstalks behind us and to the side," Mullikin told the *Dealer Sun*.

It wasn't until dogs from a nearby house ran out to intercept the beast that the teens knew they had escaped the clutches of the Crosley Monster.

That's only one encounter of many. Paranormal investigator Chris McDaniel told the *Brown County Democrat* such reports from that area are common. In 2003, a family camping in the county saw the same thing—a monstrous, hairy silhouette in the trees, like something was watching them.

CHAPTER 15
IOWA

IOWA IS KNOWN FOR corn. Lots and lots of corn. Bordered by the Missouri River to the west, and the Mississippi River to the east, this midwestern state is composed mostly of farms that spread over its vast plains and gentle hills. According to the newspaper *USA Today*, Iowa is the most American state. It has the most bald eagles per square mile, most Olympic gold medals won per capita, most native-Iowan astronauts per capita, most Major League Baseball players per capita, and the largest percentage of homes with firearms. Famous residents of Iowa include American icon John Wayne (born Marion Morrison), fellow actors Ashton Kutcher and Elijah Wood, astrophysicist James A. Van Allen, painter Grant Wood, and Otto Rohwedder, the man who invented the machine that sliced bread. Oh, and the Van Meter Monster.

VAN METER MONSTER

Van Meter Monster

For the tiny city of Van Meter, just east of Des Moines, 1903 was a year of legend. One night in October, a handful of citizens reported seeing a human-shaped monster flying with giant bat wings. On the monster's head was a horn that glowed like a searchlight, according the *Des Moines Register*. Local businessman U.G. Griffin shot at the creature as it flew over downtown businesses, but either he missed, or the bullets didn't bother the monster. A day later, a banker and the town doctor saw the monster. It stood upon the ground, and left three-toed prints.

The sightings didn't stop there. The next night, the owner of the local hardware store, O.V. White, shot at the beast as it perched on a telephone pole. Again, the shots either missed, or were ineffective.

Townspeople, armed with rifles, followed the monster to an abandoned mine outside town, and heard it scream. "The noise opened up again, as though Satan and a regiment of imps were coming forth for battle," according to a 1903 edition of the *Des Moines Daily News*.

Two monsters emerged from the mine to face the townsmen, but retreated under the firepower, and never emerged again.

Lockridge Monster

On a night in late October 1975, farmer Herb Peiffer saw a "four-legged, black-haired thing in the cornfield" near Lockridge as he drove his tractor to his turkey pens, according to an article in the *Milwaukee Sentinel*. At first, Herb didn't tell anyone about the creature he saw in his tractor lights because, according to his wife, "he thought we would make fun of him." Then Herb discovered he wasn't alone.

Local man Lowell Adkins was hunting when he discovered ten-inch tracks near the remains of four slaughtered, and partly eaten, turkeys. People thought the tracks might have been those of a black bear, although the last recorded bear sighting in Iowa was at Spirit Lake in 1876, according to the Iowa Department of Natural Resources. Although bear sightings have increased in recent years, in 1975 they were largely unheard of.

Word of a bear loose in Jefferson County kept people in their homes after dark, but further reports made them wonder about going outside at all. Lockridge resident Gloria Olsen spotted the beast one night, and she knew it wasn't a bear. "It was just before dark and I was driving past an old deserted farmyard when I saw it," Olson told reporters. "To me, it looked like it had a monkey's face and kind of had hair all over."

The Lockridge Monster is still a mystery.

Hairy Wildwoman

Hunters spotted a Wildman "of the female sex" in the forest near Gordon's Ferry, twelve miles north of Dubuque, on July 17, 1884, according to the *Dubuque Herald*. When hunters spotted the woman she stood "like a statue in a clear space." Her disheveled hair was "about three feet long, and black as jet." The men had crept up behind her, and when she realized they were there, she emitted "an unearthly scream" and ran through the woods at tremendous speed. She looked to be about twenty years old. The Wildwoman was nude; the most disturbing attribute was her receding forehead. The men searched the woods for hours but never saw her again.

Monster Turtle of Big Blue

In a thirty-four-foot-deep lake in an old rock quarry near Mason City lurks an enormous snapping turtle. Over the years, people fishing in Big Blue Pond in Clear Lake State Park claim to have seen this monster with a shell the size of a Volkswagen Beetle, according to the *Mason City Globe Gazette*.

Reports of enormous jaws that have threatened to eat swimmers have appeared from time to time, but officially the beast doesn't exist. Clear Lake State Park officials say there's no evidence to show that a snapping turtle greater than normal lives in the pond. Locals claim otherwise.

CHAPTER 16
KANSAS

THE STATE OF KANSAS is known an endless sea of golden wheat fields and prairie that stretch across the Great Plains, and it's the starting point for the movie *The Wizard of Oz* (1939), the first color motion picture release, along with that year's *Gone With the Wind*. But there's more to Kansas than wheat, grass, and ruby slippers. It's the geodetic center of North America, the Pizza Hut and White Castle restaurant franchises both began in Wichita, Reverend Sylvester Graham invented the cracker that bears his name, helium was discovered at the University of Kansas in 1905, and William Purvis and Charles Wilson invented the helicopter in Goodland in 1909. Famous Kansans include actors Roscoe "Fatty" Arbuckle, Buster Keaton, Harold Lloyd, and Dennis Hopper; automobile manufacturer Walter P. Chrysler; aviator Amelia Earhart; and NFL great Barry Sanders. The state, bordered by Missouri, Nebraska, Colorado, and Oklahoma, covers 82,277 square miles, 5.2 million acres of that covered in woodlands. Not a lot of space in Kansas for monsters, but there are a few.

101

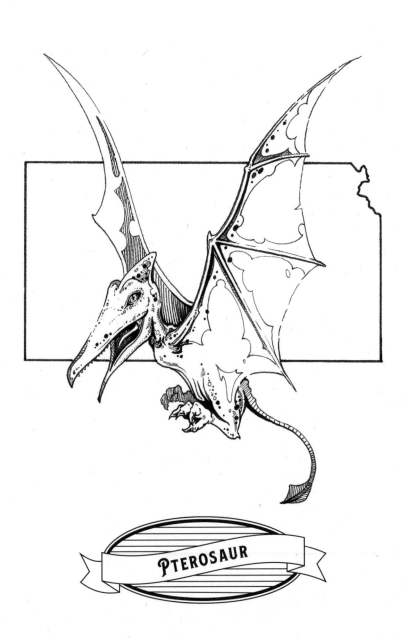

PTEROSAUR

Dogman

Michael was driving near Lawrence in August 2014 when a deer ran across the road. He slowed the car to a stop to make sure no other deer followed the first when he noticed something that froze his blood. "I saw red eyes looking at my truck," he reported to the local news. "Like eyes shine when a deer looks in a light, but just a dark red."

Michael picked up a flashlight from the cab of his vehicle and shone it toward the glowing red eyes. What he saw, he couldn't readily explain. "It was something like a dog," he said. "The back legs were shorter than the front." And it stood on its hind legs.

The animal was about the size of a Great Dane. The creature broke eye contact, and walked across the road on two legs. It took the beast three steps to cross the pavement. After it crossed, the creature dropped to four legs, ran into a field, and disappeared.

Pterosaur

In mid-2012, a husband and wife had just driven out of Hudson (population 129) when they saw what they described as a dragon, according to livepterosaur.com. "There was a row of trees alongside the road on the north," the husband said. "As we approached the end of the tree row, something huge took to the air. I said 'What the hell is that?'"

His wife told him it looked like a dragon.

This wasn't the only encounter. Sightings of flying reptiles with a wingspan of fifteen to twenty feet have been reported in Kansas over the decades. However, what the husband and wife saw that night remains a mystery.

Bigfoot

Kansas is flat (as studied scientifically by geography professors Mark Fonstad, William Pugatch, and Brandon Vogt in their 2003 paper "Kansas Is Flatter Than a Pancake" published in the journal *Annals of Improbable Research*) and is relatively forest-free (compared to bordering Colorado and Missouri), so it doesn't seem to be the most Bigfoot-friendly state. However, there are reports of the big guy stomping around the Sunflower State. According to a study at Pennsylvania State University, thirty-eight Bigfoot encounters were reported in Kansas between 1921 and 2012.

One such encounter in Cowley County was reported to the Gulf Coast Bigfoot Research Organization on September 14, 2012. The witness was on an evening run with his dog when unearthly howls split the air. He turned, and saw a "dark hairy creature" run from a tree line, then stop to look at him. "It gave the most blood-curdling screams," he reported to the GCBRO. It looked to have breasts on its chest. I believe it was a female Sasquatch."

The dog started howling and tried to run toward the creature, but the Sasquatch bolted toward another line of trees. "It was hairy from head to toe. It had distinctive breasts, and its head seemed to fit just atop its shoulders," the witness said.

Zombies

Zombies?

Although no Kansan not high on bath salts has ever reported a zombie encounter, the state is prepared for that day.

In 2014, the Kansas Division of Emergency Management announced that October was Zombie Preparedness Month, with the backing of Governor Sam Brownback.

"If you're equipped to handle the zombie apocalypse then you're prepared for tornadoes, severe storms, fire, and any other natural disaster Kansas usually faces," Devan Tucking, of the Division of Emergency Management, said.

So, to survive the zombie apocalypse, move to Kansas.

CHAPTER 17
KENTUCKY

KENTUCKY IS BEST KNOWN for its bourbon, horse racing (particularly the Kentucky Derby at Churchill Downs the first Saturday in May), and "Colonel" Harland Sanders's world famous Kentucky Fried Chicken (truth be told, Sanders lived in Indiana until he left home at age thirteen and moved to Kentucky). Famous Kentuckians include President Abraham Lincoln, boxing great Muhammad Ali, actor Johnny Depp, and famed gonzo journalist Hunter S. Thompson. The state's topography consists of mountains, farmland, rivers, coalfields, and swampy lowlands, and is the perfect place to find the Pope Lick Monster.

The Pope Lick Monster

A true "troll under the bridge" story, the Pope Lick Monster has been described as part-man/part-goat, or part-man/part-sheep, and lives beneath a railway trestle near Louisville. The monster calls for help, luring its victims onto the trestle, where they jump to their deaths before an oncoming train.

DEMON LEAPER

The origin of the monster is clouded. There are stories that it's the undead form of an old farmer who sacrificed goats to Satan, a sideshow freak, or a human-goat hybrid. Regardless of the origin, the description of the beast is consistent—it looks like a satyr from Greek mythology.

Another consistency about the monster is that the kind folks at Norfolk Southern Railway don't want the legend to drive people onto their trestle. The company has vowed to prosecute anyone caught there. Although there have been deaths from people jumping from the trestle, no one knows whether they were the despondent, thrill seekers, or victims of the Pope Lick Monster.

Herrington Lake Monster

Some people are certain there's a monster in the 2,335-acre man-made Herrington Lake. A sighting in 1972 brought the monster to the public's attention.

Lawrence Thompson was fishing in the lake when he saw something he couldn't believe. "All [I] ever seen of it is a snout, not unlike that of a pig, moving along just above the water at about the speed of a boat with a trolling motor, and a curly tail, similar to that of the same animal, coming along about fifteen feet behind," Thompson told the *Courier-Journal*. But that's all he knew about the monster. "What we don't know is colossal; what we do know is minimal," Thompson said.

Thompson's not the only one to see something monstrous in the lake. In 1990, Junction City resident Sherri Hurst saw something familiar, and terrifying, in the lake. "It was an alligator," she told *Central Kentucky News*. "I go to Florida all the time. I know what an alligator looks like, and that was an alligator."

Others suggest a catfish. Dave Baker of the State Department of Fish and Wildlife told *Central Kentucky News* there are catfish in Herrington Lake, and Kentucky grows some big ones. The largest catfish caught in the state weighed one hundred pounds.

Devil Monkeys

Three to four feet tall, excessively hairy, bipedal, and vicious, Devil Monkeys have been reported in southeastern states for decades. Resembling baboons, Devil Monkeys are also reported to have strong legs like a kangaroo, three-toed feet, and a long, bushy tail.

In Kentucky, the most famous Devil Monkey encounter occurred in 1973 when farmers near Albany reported three of these black primates had slaughtered livestock. No Devil Monkeys were ever captured. Given the fact that there are 12.4 million acres of forest in the state, it's not out of the question that a congress of baboon-like primates may have found a home in the woods of Kentucky. And yes, that's what a group of baboons is called—a congress. Makes sense.

Milton Lizard

One July day in 1975, as Clarence "Toughy" Cable walked through the wrecking yard of Blue Grass Body Shop, the business he co-owned in Milton, he saw something that shouldn't be in his state, or in his junkyard. According to the book *A Menagerie of Mysterious Beasts: Encounters with Cryptid Creatures* by Ken Gerhard, Cable saw a lizard at least fifteen feet long. The thing came from behind a wrecked car and hissed at him. The beast had eyes like a frog's; black and white stripes and dots decorated its body. Toughy's brother Garrett saw it in the wrecking yard sometime later that day.

The lizard seemed to live there. Toughy again encountered the lizard the next day and threw a rock at it; it slithered away. Toughy hurried off and brought back his rifle, firing on the lizard the next time it appeared. He couldn't tell if he hit it. A search party formed and searched for the creature, but never found it.

After Toughy reported these encounters, he was shown pictures of various lizards and said his beast looked the most like a monitor lizard. After the encounters in July, the lizard was never seen again. Toughy suggested the lizard may have come as an egg in one of the junk cars they brought to the lot from somewhere in the Southwest.

Could the Milton sightings have been of a giant monitor lizard?

Monitor lizards are native to Africa, Asia, Indonesia, and Australia. Although they now exist in the Americas, they are not native. There are seventy-nine species of monitor lizard; however, the largest, the Komodo dragon of Indonesia, reaches a length of eight-and-a-half feet. The only monitor lizard to ever achieve the size of the one Toughy encountered, the Megalania, has been extinct for fifty thousand years.

The Kentucky Mothman

The 1966 and 1967 Mothman encounters in and around the town of Point Pleasant, West Virginia, were made famous in John Keel's book *The Mothman Prophecies*, and the 2002 movie of the same name. These sightings of Mothman are related to the collapse of the Silver Bridge in 1967, which killed forty-six people. More than one hundred people claimed to have seen Mothman around Point Pleasant in those two years.

However, encounters with a Mothman-like creature aren't limited to West Virginia. In 1938, residents of Ashland and Elizabethtown, Kentucky, reported seeing a large, black, humanlike being with a huge wingspan, and blazing red eyes. Although the sightings died out by 1939, they reappeared in 2008 when a farmer said he saw a bird-like monster with red eyes near his barn. The farmer said the monster chased him.

Mothman has been considered an omen of doom. When it disappeared from Kentucky in 1939, people thought it was a precursor to war in Europe. In 1967 it foretold the collapse of the Silver Bridge. What did it foretell in 2008? The spate of tornadoes that ripped through the US? The earthquakes in China and Japan? The hurricane that devastated Haiti? It all depends on whom you ask.

The Demon Leaper

For decades upon decades, residents of Louisville would look upon the Gothic Walnut Street Baptist Church, and see what looked like a living gargoyle amongst the stone beasts. Kentucky author David Dominé told *Wave 3 News*, "It's a bat-like creature with leathery skin, wings and claws and talons and it's been seen to hop along the roof."

This gargoyle not only jumps across the rooftop, it has wings, and can fly. "It's been seen on other structures' roof tops as well. They call it the Demon Leaper. It's perhaps our most famous legend in Old Louisville," Dominé told the *Wave*.

Some witnesses claimed the Leaper was a monkey wearing a "shiny suit," and said it would leap down upon people and poke them, although no one was ever seriously injured. A September 12, 1880 story in *The New York Times* referred to the beast as "An Aerial Mystery."

Hopkinsville Goblins

The encounter started with a spaceship. Billy Ray Taylor and his wife, June, were visiting the farmhouse of Elmer "Lucky" Sutton in Christian County on August 21, 1955, when something otherworldly happened, according to an article in the *Evansville Courier and Press*.

Billy had gone outside to fetch water from the farm's well and saw a shiny flying object descend into a gully about a quarter-mile away. He rushed back inside to tell the four adults and seven children in the house, but his story was met with laughter. The laughter wouldn't last.

Soon after the excitement settled, the Sutton's dog began to bark. Lucky and Billy grabbed rifles and went to see what was upsetting the animal. They couldn't believe what they saw. A bipedal creature about three feet tall walked toward them from the darkness, its arms raised in a gesture of peace. The creature's skin was green. It had large eyes, a large mouth and enormous ears; its spindly hands ended in claws.

Billy did what any country boy would have done in 1955—he took a shot at it. They couldn't tell if Billy had hit the creature (although he shot at close range), but after the shot, the little green man did a back flip and disappeared into the trees. That wasn't the last they saw of it.

As soon as the men walked into the house, they saw the green man, or a similar one, staring at them through the window. The men shot again, but when they went outside to take a look at the thing, it was gone. No sooner had their shock at the thing's disappearance began to fade than a clawed hand reached at them from the edge of the roof. The men shot toward the roof but missed the creature. The little green man floated into the air, landed on the ground nearby, and dashed into the forest. The men hurried back into the house.

The green things didn't leave them alone. They kept popping up in windows all around the house, only to be targeted by Lucky and Billy's weapons. The men never dropped one of the creatures, but they shot holes in the walls.

When it seemed like the creatures had gone, they all rushed to their vehicle and tore into Hopkinsville to get help from the law. The sheriff's department responded to the Sutton house, but all deputies found were numerous bullet holes in the walls and window screens. Officers stayed until 2:15 a.m.

An hour and fifteen minutes later, the creatures returned.

Although the case was investigated by Hopkinsville Police, the county sheriff's office, the state patrol, and the military, no proof of the little green men was ever found. That hasn't stopped the nearby unincorporated Christian County community of Kelly from celebrating the event with the annual Little Green Men Days.

CHAPTER 18
LOUISIANA

NAMED AFTER FRENCH KING Louis XIV, Louisiana (Land of Louis) is a hodgepodge of cultures, a mixing of French, African, Spanish, and American. Claimed as a French territory by explorer Robert Cavelier de La Salle in 1682, it changed hands to the fledgling United States in 1803. It is birthplace of the National Football League's Manning brothers, musician Louis Armstrong, and *Suicide Squad*'s Joker, Jared Leto. The state's geography is split into two parts: the lower alluvial region of swamps, marshes, and tiny islands where the Mississippi River flows into the Gulf of Mexico; and the northern part of the state, which is composed mainly of prairies, hills, and forests. All great hiding places for beasts like the Rougaru.

The Rougaru

This humanlike monster with the head of a wolf prowls the swamps and streets of small-town Louisiana looking for human prey. Louisiana's early French settlers brought stories of the

GRUNCH

loup-garou (French for werewolf), and maybe the werewolves themselves. The Rougaru is a cursed man who must turn into part wolf for a year and a day, or until transferring the curse to another by a bite, or by simply not talking about it. Appearing sickly in human form, the Rougaru is a large, ferocious beast when it changes. It is nearly ten feet tall, with dark fur, and fiery red eyes.

Some legends claim the monster maintains human form until it can lure an unsuspecting victim into an isolated place, where it turns into a wolf man. Other legends have this Louisiana werewolf hunting Catholics who don't observe Lent.

The Grunch

Based in eastern New Orleans, the Grunch is a group of small humans that live in the woods, on a dead-end road on the outskirts of the city. Having interbred for decades, these albino dwarves are stunted, and appear barely human. The Grunch also have a taste for blood. Area farmers talk about missing goats and other small livestock, only to later find them dead, and drained of blood.

Some say the deaths attributed to the Grunch are really caused by local predators; others blame the Chupacabra. Although a terrifying tale told by local teens before they cruise out to Grunch Road at night, these Louisiana goatsuckers are similar to Melon Head reports from around the country.

Sea Monster

Newspapers in the 1800s were rife with tales of water monsters in North America. Louisiana wasn't any different. In 1856, a Louisiana newspaper reported that a local man named Martial Ogeron killed a "monster" in the Bayou Lafourche in the southeastern part of the state, according to "Regional Sea Stories—Close Encounter With A Creature of the Finny Tribe" by Brasseaux and Hoese.

Ogeron encountered the sea monster at the mouth of the Bayou Lafourche, where it was eating small fish on the bottom of the river. Ogeron shot the monster in the head, hooked a rope to it, and towed it to shore. The fisherman estimated the beast to be fourteen feet long with a six-foot tail, and a three-foot, six-inch mouth. Ogeron had begun to butcher the animal when a storm hit. Its skin resembled "more that of an elephant than anything else to which we can compare it," and its liver "was the size of a rice cask."

The storm increased to the point Ogeron had to abandon his catch and find shelter. After the storm abated, Ogeron discovered the monster had been washed away. Historians speculate the monster could have been a manta ray, or a manatee.

Honey Island Swamp Monster

In 1963, a retired air traffic controller began the legend of a large, hairy, bipedal creature in Honey Island Swamp, a 108.1-square-mile wildlife refuge filled with snakes, alligators, and maybe monsters. Honey Island itself, named because of a once impressive population of honeybees on a nearby island, is between fifteen and twenty miles long, and between three and seven miles wide. It is covered in heavy timber. The retired controller Harland Ford claims to have seen the monster when fishing in the area, according to *Country Roads Magazine*. He quickly left and brought back a friend, Bill Mills, and made plaster casts of the beast's footprints—the feet had three webbed toes. Debunkers claim those footprints were left by an alligator, but the prints were almost too large for a gator.

Ford wasn't the only one to see the creature. Local man Ted Williams (not the Hall of Fame baseball player) saw it multiple times. In a television interview, Williams said the monster was about seven feet tall, and covered in dark gray hair. The creature jumped into the swamp when it realized Williams was watching it. In another instance, Williams claims to have seen two of the beasts, with "broad shoulders, arms hanging down below their knees, hands looked almost like a human's."

One of the local legends about the tall, hairy, manlike creature involved a train wreck at the turn of the twentieth century, when a number of circus chimpanzees supposedly escaped, and bred with alligators.

The last official sighting of the monster was in 1974.

CHAPTER 19
MAINE

THE STATE OF MAINE sits at the top northeastern point of the US. One of the smaller states (thirty-ninth), and also one of the least populated (forty-first), Maine is considered the safest state in the country in terms of crime. Maine can claim earmuffs (they were invented there), the world's largest rotating globe (Eartha is more than forty-one feet in diameter), and poet Henry Wadsworth Longfellow. Filled with forested parks, low mountains, picturesque lakes, and lined by rocky coastlines, it is not only one of the most beautiful states in the union, it's also home to quite a few monsters. Given the fact that horror author Stephen King is from Maine, it may actually be home to all the monsters—ever.

Cassie

The monster nicknamed Cassie was first seen in Penobscot Bay in 1779, when future US Navy hero Edward Preble (just an ensign at the time) aboard the ship the *Protector* saw a sea serpent

SPECTER MOOSE

on the surface of the water. On closer examination, the creature stirred, and raised its head about ten feet out of the water before diving into the depths and disappearing, according to a story in the *Bangor Daily News*. A similar sighting was reported the next year in Broad Bay, when sailors observed a serpent about forty-five feet long raise its head out of the water on a long skinny neck before diving out of sight.

Cassie has been seen all along the coast of Maine, many times from 1912 to the 1940s. In 1958, fisherman Ole Mikkelsen saw a hundred-foot-long serpent with a large head, and a tail like a fish. The creature seemed to watch Mikkelsen and a fellow fisherman as they spread their fishing nets, before it swam away.

The last reported sighting was in 2002 by a woman who wished to remain anonymous. She called a science museum claiming to have seen something near Biddeford that looked like the Loch Ness Monster.

Pocomoonshine Lake Monster

The Algonquian Indians of Maine have seen a monster in Pocomoonshine Lake for centuries. Legend has it the monster is a result of a disagreement between an Algonquin shaman and a chief of the Micmac. The Micmac chief turned into an enormous serpent, which the shaman vanquished and tied to a tree next to the lake. Since then a serpentlike creature nearly sixty feet long has been seen swimming in the lake.

However, unlike Cassie, this monster isn't confined to the water. The Pocomoonshine Lake Monster has been reported to be able to leave the lake, and drag its gigantic body across land to nearby lakes. A sawmill owner claimed to have seen the Pocomoonshine Lake Monster's trail in 1882. The man said the monster's track was four feet wide, and three feet deep.

The White Monkey

First seen in the 1500s, the White Monkey (as Europeans called it) of Saco River has lurked in the areas around the river for centuries. Described as a white-skinned man with webbed fingers, the White Monkey may be the result of a curse laid upon Europeans when a group of drunks kidnapped an indigenous woman and her child, and threw them off Saco Falls. The tribe's shaman cursed the waters, and the White Monkey reportedly killed three white men each year. Although the White Monkey was last seen in the 1970s, the most famous sighting was by a twelve-year-old Joseph Smith, founder of the Mormon Church in the 1800s, according to etravelmaine.com.

Specter Moose

A giant white moose weighing nearly 2,500 pounds, standing fifteen feet tall, and having antlers that stretch ten feet, has been sighted around Bangor for more than one hundred years. In comparison, an average male moose can weigh about 990 pounds, stand around six feet tall, and have an antler span of around six feet.

Called the Specter Moose because of its color, hunters have sought this enormous moose since the 1890s. Sightings of the Specter Moose were reported in 1917, and again in 1999.

Bigfoot

Bigfoot sightings in Maine stretch back to the 1800s. The first account, published in the book *Camping Out* by C.A. Stevens, involves a trapper who was "ripped apart" by a creature. Although some people suspected a mountain lion, the trapper's body had been beaten against a tree.

According to a story in the *Bangor Daily News*, in 1895, two women and three boys picking blueberries saw a bipedal creature that "looked like an immense African monkey." In 1942, two sisters were fishing in Meddybemps Lake when two "hair-covered giants" stole their fish. Sightings of the "Durham Gorilla" began in July 1973, and lasted until mid-August. The sightings began when a group of boys riding bicycles saw something they thought looked like a giant chimpanzee.

Wendigo

This creature is an Algonquian Indian legend that involves a malevolent spirit that possesses a human body, and gives the person a taste for human flesh. Depicted as everything from a hairy human with sharp teeth and bulging eyes, to an emaciated humanlike creature with antlers, to an ice giant that moves in a whirlwind, the one constant in all Wendigo legends is that it is a cannibal. People are susceptible to Wendigo possession if they are cursed or have resorted to cannibalism during a famine.

CHAPTER 20
MARYLAND

THE STATE OF MARYLAND, recognized as the birthplace of religious freedom in the New World, is the ninth-smallest state in the Union at 12,406.68 square miles. However, that's still larger than the entire country of Belgium. Although small, it has a lot of shoreline. According to the National Oceanic and Atmospheric Administration, Maryland has the tenth-longest tidal shoreline in the US, at 3,190 miles. The lyrics of the national anthem of the United States, "The Star-Spangled Banner," are taken from the poem "Defence of Fort M'Henry" (yes, that's how it's spelled), written by attorney Francis Scott Key during the battle at Maryland's Fort McHenry during the War of 1812. The state is the birthplace of baseball legend Babe Ruth, civil rights leader Harriet Tubman, and *Baywatch* star (and German singing sensation) David Hasselhoff. It's also home to something called the Snallygaster.

SNALLYGASTER

Snallygaster

As early as the 1700s, Maryland residents claimed a giant reptilian bird soared through the skies above the state. The ravenous creature would swoop down and pluck pets, game, livestock, and sometimes children from the ground, disappearing with them into the skies. According to an article in the *Baltimore Sun*, Ed Okonowicz, author of the book *Monsters of Maryland*, said German immigrants brought stories of the Snallygaster here with them, and maybe the monster itself.

"Among the most distinctive creatures to settle in and hide among the wooded niches of America's eastern mountains and valleys is the Snallygaster—a fearsome, dragon-like flying beast," Okonowicz wrote in his book *Monsters of Maryland*. Eyewitness descriptions of the Snallygaster sound like that of a pterosaur; an enormous flying monster with a wingspan of twenty-five to thirty feet, a long beak, and leathery skin that looks like a reptile. However, the Snallygaster also has tentacles, talons of steel, and carries with it the pungent scent of death. Its shriek resembles a train whistle.

Reports of the Snallygaster in Maryland continued until the 1930s, when they became sporadic, appearing again in 1948 and 1973. A local man named James Harding was the first to lay claim to a Snallygaster sighting, describing the monster as having one eye in the center of its forehead.

The Goatman

What is it with goats? Kentucky has its own legend of a goatman, as do Texas and Missouri. So does Maryland. Prince George's County, so close to the nation's capital of Washington, DC, that residents can smell the corruption, is the home of a half-man/half-goat monster straight out of a horror movie.

Reports of an ax-wielding satyr-like creature chasing automobiles near Beltsville stretch through the years. According to an article in *Modern Farmer*, the goatman legend has numerous beginnings. Either the entity was a goat farmer seeking revenge on teenagers who killed his livestock, a monster created by the Beltsville Agricultural Research Center, or a natural monster native to the area. The *Modern Farmer* article quotes University of Maryland professor Dr. Barry Pearson who said goatman sightings began in the 1950s, and became frantically popular in the 1970s.

A *Washington Post* story in 1971 about the death of a pet included quotes from locals blaming the goatman. If the goatman killed that pet, he must have been really maa-maa-mad.

Chessie

Chesapeake Bay, the largest estuary (a partially enclosed body of water attached to an ocean and fed by rivers) in the United States, is 64,299 square miles of water that stretches from southern Virginia to northern Maryland. It's also the home of Chessie.

This sea monster is described as a dark, snakelike creature about thirty feet long that seems to simply watch people working or playing in the bay. Although seen for decades, the first solid photographic evidence came in 1982 when a family videotaped Chessie from Kent Island, Maryland, the largest island in Chesapeake Bay. The tape shows an animal fitting Chessie's description. Same shape, same length.

Although most sightings of this creature occurred in the 1970s and 1980s, they continue today.

The Sykesville Monster

Bigfoot was popular in the United States in the 1970s. Missouri's Momo, Louisiana's Honey Island Swamp Monster, Arkansas's Fouke Monster—all were spotted in that decade. Maryland was no exception. Enter the Sykesville Monster.

In 1973, the area around Sykesville, northwest of Baltimore, was stalked by a Bigfoot-like creature, with reports of encounters so terrifying that it was hunted by "police, a game warden, zoo officials, and professional paranormal investigators," according to the *Carroll County Times*. Police took a plaster cast of a footprint that was thirteen inches long and seven inches wide.

Author and researcher Lon Strickler, who posts his work at phantomsandmonsters.com, became interested in cryptozoology on a May morning in 1981 when he saw the Sykesville Monster.

Strickler was fly-fishing in the Patapsco River near Sykesville when he noticed a dog wandering the banks. The dog simply sniffed the weeds near the water, and Strickler ignored it until the dog began to bark and growl. Strickler looked up and saw a hair-covered bipedal creature about eight feet tall standing in a thicket. Strickler froze and observed the monster. The monster made a ticking sound and smelled like fox urine. As Strickler moved to get a better look at the creature, it walked away.

Strickler returned to his vehicle, drove into town, and called the police. Within an hour the area was filled with people hunting for the creature. They never found it.

CHAPTER 21
MASSACHUSETTS

ONE OF THE ORIGINAL thirteen British colonies in North America, Massachusetts was pivotal in the American Revolution. It is the third most densely populated of the fifty states and the seventh smallest. It's the birthplace of printer, author, inventor, and political theorist Benjamin Franklin; President John F. Kennedy; authors Theodor "Dr. Seuss" Geisel and Edgar Allan Poe; and Captain America Chris Evans. The state has coastal and interior lowlands, several large bays, and residual mountains. A two-hundred-square-mile area called "the Bridgewater Triangle" in the southeastern part of the state is home to UFO encounters, ghosts, animal mutilation, and Bigfoot reports. Oh, and don't forget the Pukwudgie.

Pukwudgie

Many Native American mythologies have stories of little people. The Wampanoag of Massachusetts's legend is of the Pukwudgie. Jealous of the affection the Wampanoag showed the giant

PUKWUDGIE

Maushop (well, the giant *did* create Cape Cod for them), the Pukwudgie began to torment the Wampanoag Indians, playing tricks on them, stealing their children, and burning their villages. Pukwudgies are described as humanlike, two to three feet tall, with large noses and ears. Their skin is gray.

The Pukwudgie can become invisible, use magic, and create fire at the snap of their fingers, but their most dangerous antics involve shooting poison arrows (with which legend says they used to kill Maushop and his five sons) and turning into a half-porcupine/half-troll. These diminutive humanlike monsters have been known to lure humans to their deaths either by poison arrow, or pushing the human off a cliff. Afterward, the Pukwudgie can control the souls of their victims.

In modern times, people have reported encountering Pukwudgies in Freetown-Fall River State Forest, which includes a reservation in the Wampanoag Nation.

Thunderbird

Another Native American legend, the Thunderbird is an enormous bird whose name comes from the thunderous beating of its giant wings. Seen over the centuries across the continent, the Thunderbird closely resembles a family of birds called the teratorns that existed between the Miocene and Pleistocene periods. These monster birds (teratorn is Greek for just that, "monster bird") had wingspans of eleven to twenty feet and weighed anywhere from thirty-three to 176 pounds. Native American stories of these flying terrors across North America are eerily similar. Thunderbirds can create storms and shoot lightning bolts. They have been known to swoop low and scoop up children and animals.

Sightings of Thunderbirds have occurred all over Massachusetts, including this one from Easton as reported in the *Boston Globe* from a story written by cryptozoologist Loren Coleman. According to the article, police sergeant Thomas Dowdy was driving home from his shift during the summer in 1971 when a bird about six feet tall with wings twelve feet long lifted from the side of the road and soared over his vehicle and disappeared into the night.

An account on about.com by an anonymous author who posted as "Bob" involved what he thought was a hang glider in the sky around dusk one autumn in 1995, near Weston. Bob drove over a hill and saw the "glider" heading straight toward his vehicle. Bob slammed the brakes and saw something he couldn't believe. The flying object wasn't a glider; it was a bird with a wingspan of around twenty feet.

According to a story at cryptozoologynews.com, in August of 2015, two men working near Blandford saw a huge bird they thought at first was a small airplane. They realized it was not an airplane when it began to flap its wings.

Dover Demon

For a few days in the spring of 1977, the town of Dover was terrorized by a demon. At around 10:30 p.m. on April 21, seventeen-year-old Billy Bartlett saw a four-foot-tall humanoid creature standing near a wall on Farm Street. The creature had a head like a watermelon, and glowing orange eyes, but no mouth or nose. Bartlett told the *Boston Globe* in 2006 that the demon was real. "I have no idea what it was," Bartlett told the *Globe*. "I definitely know I saw something."

Five more witnesses came out claiming to have seen the demon in 1977, including fifteen-year-old John Baxter, who stood within fifteen feet of the monster on Miller Hill Road at 12:30 a.m. as he walked home from his girlfriend's house. The next day, fifteen-year-old Abby Brabham saw the demon sitting on Springdale Avenue.

Carl Sheridan, a former police chief in Dover, told the *Globe* the story has always bothered him. "I knew the kids involved. They were good kids ... The whole thing was unusual."

Beast of Truro

During the autumn of 1981, pets and livestock were slaughtered by an unknown creature around Truro, a small town on the northern tip of Cape Cod. The first victims were dozens of cats found torn apart in an area of the small town. Various deaths continued through 1981 and into 1982, when hogs were found injured, their "flanks ripped by deep claw marks," according to a story in the *New York Times*. People suspected a pack of wild dogs until the sightings began. Locals reported seeing a "large furry creature that they did not recognize," according to the *Times*.

The clearest sighting was by a married couple from Truro, William and Marsha Medeiros, who were taking a walk near Head of the Meadow Beach. "It had a very definite long rope-like tail like the letter J," Marsha Medeiros told the *Times*. "We figured it was about as tall as up to our knees and weighed sixty or eighty pounds." The animal had a catlike face and short ears. Marsha Medeiros was convinced they had seen a mountain lion.

Others also reported seeing something that looked like a mountain lion, although the last reported mountain lion in

Massachusetts was in 1858. Despite numerous sightings, footprints were never found. Eventually the sightings, and animal deaths, faded.

Gloucester Sea Serpent

The first report of the hundred-foot-long serpent in the harbor of Gloucester occurred in 1638, when British traveler and author John Josselyn wrote the tale of a "sea serpent, or snake, that lay quoiled [sic] up like a cable upon the rock at Cape Ann; a boat passing by with English on board, and two Indians, they would have shot the serpent, but the Indians dissuaded them, saying that if he were not killed outright, they would all be in danger of their lives."

In 1817, fishermen claimed to see a snakelike reptilian beast with the head of a horse and a foot-long horn from the center of its head. It poked its head above the surface of the harbor, and looked around before sinking back into the depths. That was by no means the last sighting. Two women claimed to see the creature on August 10, 1817. By 1818, seamen and clergymen said they saw the monster.

Sightings have continued through the decades. Although the number of encounters has decreased over the years, two of note occurred in the 1960s and in 1997.

CHAPTER 22
MICHIGAN

BORDERING FOUR OF THE five Great Lakes, home to 64,980 inland bodies of water, and heavily forested in the north, Michigan is popular with hunters and fishermen. The southern part of the state is home to Detroit, center of the United States automobile industry. Michigan is the largest state by area east of the Mississippi River, and has the tenth-largest population. It has more lighthouses, registered boats, and public golf courses than any other state. Famous people born in Michigan include singers Stevie Wonder and Iggy Pop, NBA great Earvin "Magic" Johnson, tennis player Serena Williams (her sister Venus was born in California), actor Terry Crews, car manufacturer and entrepreneur Henry Ford, and lots of monsters.

Nain Rouge

When the founder of the city of Detroit, Antoine de la Mothe Cadillac, first traveled to the area in 1701, he was attacked by a monster. The creature was a small, manlike beast with flaming

MISHIPESHU

red eyes, rotten teeth, and reddish-black fur all over its body. The local Native American people, the Ottawa, knew this dwarf as their protector. However, when the French settled the area, they felt it cursed the city and viewed it as a symbol of death, according to the *Detroit Metro Times*.

The Nain Rouge, "red dwarf" in French, was seen dancing amongst the corpses of the fifty-eight British soldiers killed by the Ottawa tribe on Parent's Creek in the Battle of Bloody Run during Pontiac's Rebellion, July 30, 1763. The battle was so bloody, eyewitnesses claimed Parent's Creek turned red for days.

People saw the Nain Rouge days before a fire claimed most of the city of Detroit in 1805, and again when General William Hull surrendered Fort Detroit to the British in the War of 1812. More reports of the Nain Rouge came throughout the 1800s, usually before a death, and into the 1900s. People caught glimpses of the dwarf in the days before the 12th Street Riot in 1967, and before the huge ice storm of 1976 when two utility workers thought they saw a child climbing a pole, but were terrified to discover it was the red dwarf.

Today, the Nain Rouge is commemorated by the locally-brewed beer "Detroit Dwarf Lager," and with a parade.

Mishipeshu

The Mishipeshu, or "the Great Lynx," is a water creature that appears in the mythology of many Native American tribes of the Upper Midwest. Although it has the head and paws of a great cat, it also has the antlers of a deer, a body covered in reptilian scales with spikes running along the backbone, and a long, snakelike tail. The roar of the Mishipeshu sounds like running rapids. The

Great Lynx lives in the deepest parts of lakes, and sometimes rivers, and often brings storms.

The Mishipeshu guards the copper deposits that surround Lake Superior. Any copper removed angers the Mishipeshu, and it has been known to sink boats in its fury.

A story told by a Jesuit missionary in the 1600s involves four Ojibwa Indians who paddled to Michipicoten Island (home of the Mishipeshu) to get copper. As soon as the Indians put their boat back into the water with the copper, the Mishipeshu attacked the boat from underneath, killing three of the four Indians. The fourth crawled home to tell the tale.

Michigan Mermen

The Maymaygwashi is another Ojibwa water legend. The Maymaygwashi live in rocky cracks along the banks of Lake Superior, and in forest waterways. These creatures resemble children with hair-covered faces. French-Canadian trappers and fishermen who wandered the areas around the Great Lakes claimed to have seen the Maymaygwashi.

In 1812, traveling in Lake Superior with three Ojibwa Indians by canoe, a French-Canadian fisherman named Saint-Germain was camped at an island for the night when he saw a creature in the lake that had the upper torso "of a child of eight. The face had a dark complexion and curly hair." The lower body still in the water "seemed to be that of a fish." Saint-Germain tried to shoot the merman, but the Ojibwa wouldn't let him.

Later that night a storm struck the island and didn't abate for three days. The Indians blamed the storm on Saint-Germain's rash act.

The Dogman

Towering six to seven feet tall, the Michigan Dogman is a wolf-like creature that is said to walk—and run—on its hind legs. The Dogman was first seen in 1887 when two lumberjacks encountered the monster, according to an article in the *Huffington Post.*

More Dogman sightings began in 1928 in Paris, Michigan, when seventeen-year-old Robert Fortney was charged by a pack of wild dogs. He fired a shot over the pack's head, but when the pack ran at the sound, one huge black dog with blue eyes stood its ground. Fortney shot another round over the beast's head, then the monster stood on two legs and stared down Fortney until it turned and disappeared into the woods.

Similar reports have arisen through the years since the 1950s, like the encounters by S. Costea and his family near Romulus.

As a child Costea lived in a farmhouse with his mother, his uncle, and his mother's boyfriend. Woods separated the house from a nearby major road, woods that kept the house and the family hidden. Something terrifying lived in those woods. "We had this really strange dog creature that would hang around the property," Costea said. "I say dog creature because this thing was far too big and intelligent to be a stray dog." The animal, as big as a Great Dane, seemed to have the upper part of a German Shepherd and the lower part a Doberman pinscher—it also had red eyes.

"It seemed to have no fear," Costea said. "My uncle would yell at it or throw things toward it to try to scare it off but it would simply rear up on its hind legs like a ram and charge at (him) for a short distance."

The family would find its chickens and rabbits torn to bits and screens often torn from doors and windows. Then one day this dog-thing spoke. "One summer night my mom had left the window open in my bedroom to cool the room off so I could sleep," Costea said. "She was on her way to the bathroom and went by my room and heard me talking to someone."

Stopping by her son's door, well after his bedtime, she thought he was playing. She opened the bedroom door, turned on the lights, and saw the dog. "When she opened the door she saw me standing in my bed and I had apparently wet my pajamas," he said. "I was talking toward the window. I wasn't screaming or freaking out but seemed to be transfixed and talking in a low voice toward the window... The dog had its two front paws pushed through the screen and was looking through the window at us and making a low growl." Costea's mother threw the bottle she carried into the beast's face and it backed out of the window. She slammed the window shut and closed the blinds.

Eventually Costea's uncle shot the beast, and although he didn't kill it, the Dogman never bothered the family again.

Sea Monsters

About six hundred feet from shore near the Straits of Mackinac that connect Lakes Michigan and Huron, people witnessed two unknown creatures in the water in June 1976. According to the *Grand Rapids Press,* the local sheriff came to the spot on the beach where people saw the monsters, and he saw something he'd never seen before. "I'm looking at something twenty, maybe thirty feet long, swimming just below the surface," he told the *Grand Rapids Press.* "I was amazed. I didn't know what it was, but it sure wasn't a publicity stunt." The creature would occasionally rise to the surface of the water before diving back into the depths.

According to the article, the creature could have been an enormous fish, or eel, although the reported length of maybe thirty feet makes that unlikely.

Dewey Lake Monster

In 1964, people around Dewey Lake began seeing a hairy, ten-foot-tall, five-hundred-pound apelike creature lumbering through a fifteen-mile area of swamp near Decatur. A Bigfoot? Maybe, but witnesses claimed it swam underwater, had scales on some parts of its body, and had claws like a bear.

Once the stories of these encounters began to hit the media, thousands of people flocked to the Dewey Lake area searching for the beast. It was never found. However, it's still being seen. And it's apparently angrier that it was in 1964.

"Some of these reports have smashed cars, turned over cars. That's scary. Seeing something would be scary enough but being aggressed by some sort of unknown creature would be incredibly [frightening]," Wendy Alexander, a resident of the area, told WWMT Newschannel 3.

Many people have recently reported encounters with the Dewey Lake Monster, including visual accounts, damaged property, and large footprints.

CHAPTER 23
MINNESOTA

MINNESOTA IS, IN A word, beautiful. From its vast cornfields that sprawl over the rolling hills in the southern part of the state, to the lush forests of the north, every inch of Minnesota looks like a greeting card. Then there are the lakes, 11,842 of them, making the state a hunting and fishing paradise. The name Minnesota is a Dakota Indian word that means "clear blue water." Famous residents include authors F. Scott Fitzgerald and Sinclair Lewis, actress and singer Judy Garland, *Peanuts* creator Charles Shulz, and singer-songwriters Prince and Bob Dylan. With 60 percent of the residents of Minnesota living in and around the Minneapolis-Saint Paul region, that leaves a lot of the state sparsely populated, and a haven for creatures to lurk.

WENDIGO

Minnesota Iceman

Although whether the Minnesota Iceman was real or a hoax is still debated, the fact is that something frozen and apelike existed and was carted around as a sideshow attraction throughout North America through the 1960s and 1970s.

Carnival show promoter Frank Hansen claimed this six-foot-tall, humanlike creature was found in Siberia. The thing had an apelike face, a broken arm, and a bullet hole in the back of its head. Famed cryptozoologists Ivan T. Sanderson and Bernard Heuvelmans examined the Iceman at Hansen's home in Minnesota. They were convinced it was a genuine biological specimen, complete with a rotting odor in spots where the ice had melted, according to *Scientific American*. An article on the Iceman appeared in a European scientific journal labeling it a new species of Neanderthal, which prompted Hansen to tout it in traveling fairs as the missing link, charging looky-loos twenty-five cents to gaze upon the creature.

Then things get fuzzy. Hansen claimed he'd hidden away the original Iceman because it was becoming damaged with all the travel, and began using for the show a model of the Iceman covered in latex and hair. Soon after, the Smithsonian Institution declared the Minnesota Iceman a hoax.

You can see the latex one yourself, if you'd like. The Minnesota Iceman is on display in the Museum of the Weird in Austin, Texas.

The Mystery Monster

In 2011, Lacey Ilse stopped her vehicle near Alexandria (population: small) because of an unidentifiable lump on the shoulder of the road. Ilse told the *Minneapolis Star-Tribune* the thing was "ghostly white and hairless, its neck bloated out of proportion with the rest of its limp body." She also told the newspaper it looked "half human."

Locals thought the Mystery Monster might be a hairless badger, dog, raccoon, or a wolf. Others thought it was a bizarre government experiment escaped from a lab, or was the legendary Chupacabra. Eventually, the Minnesota Department of Natural Resources (notorious party poopers) said the dead beast was probably a decaying badger.

But there is some hope the Mystery Monster was just that, a mystery monster. "Probably" is not "certainly."

Pepie

Lake Pepin, part of the Mississippi River system and split by Minnesota and Wisconsin, sits about sixty miles downstream of Minneapolis-Saint Paul, and has a surface area of forty square miles. Although the lake is only twenty-one feet deep, some think that's deep enough to be home to a monster.

Local man Larry Nielson, who operates the paddlewheel boat *Pearl of the Lake*, saw something on Lake Pepin, according to the *Star-Tribune*. Nielson saw a wake that was about two hundred feet long and two feet high, going upstream. He couldn't explain it.

Pepie has its roots in history. According to newspaper accounts, in the 1600s a Frenchman, Father Louis Hennepin, claimed to see "a huge serpent as big as a man's leg and seven or eight feet long" in the area where the lake is now.

Locals have speculated that Pepie could be anything from a sturgeon, to an alligator gar, to a surviving plesiosaur.

Whether Pepie exists or not, Lake City, which sits on the shores of Lake Pepin, at least has the title of "the birthplace of water skiing." The sport was invented there in 1922 by Ralph Samuelson.

The Wendigo

Although I covered the Wendigo in Maine, apparently this big fella really gets around. The Wendigo is a creature that was once a man who ate another human. This unforgivable sin transforms a human into a fifteen-foot-tall shaggy monster with long fangs and glowing yellow eyes. Oh, and it's hungry, too. Always hungry—for human flesh.

The early white settlers in Minnesota claimed to have seen these wicked banshees and considered them an omen of death. Reportedly in the late 1800s to the early 1900s, the town of Roseau, eleven miles south of the Canadian border, had a number of sightings of a Wendigo; each sighting was followed by a death.

Sightings of this creature in northern Minnesota and Canada are still reported.

CHAPTER 24
MISSISSIPPI

THE FIRST EUROPEAN TO set foot in Mississippi was the Spanish explorer Hernando de Soto, who discovered the Mississippi River in 1540. The first European settlement, however, was constructed by the French in 1699. Not to be embarrassed by the Spanish and French, the British took over what is now Mississippi in 1763, only to give it to the fledgling United States after the Revolutionary War. The state ranks in the low thirties in size and population, but what it doesn't have in land and people, it makes up for in catfish. Mississippi is the leading producer of farm-raised catfish, not just in the United States, but in the world. Its geography consists of low hills, farmland, forests, swamp, and coastline. Famous Mississippians include author William Faulkner; playwright Tennessee Williams; musicians Elvis Presley, B.B. King, Muddy Waters, Howlin' Wolf, John Lee Hooker, and Bo Diddley; NFL greats Walter Payton, Jerry Rice, and Brett Favre; talk show host Oprah Winfrey; Muppets creator Jim Henson; civil rights activist Ruby Bridges; and, quite

PASCAGOULA RIVER ALIEN

possibly the greatest voice on the planet, James Earl Jones (Darth Vader). Gallup polls show Mississippi to be the most religious state in the country, probably because people are trying to pray away all those monsters.

Mississippi Mermaid

The Pascagoula River meanders eighty miles through southeastern Mississippi, eventually draining into the Mississippi Sound. Once home to the Pascagoula Indians, it is now home to mermaids. The legend of the Mississippi Mermaid is also that of the Singing River, as the Pascagoula is also called. According to the website of the Smithsonian Institution, Anola, a princess of the Biloxi tribe, was in love with Altama, Chief of the Pascagoula tribe. When the Biloxi chieftain, angered by this affair, led his tribe to war against the nearby Pascagoula, the peaceful Pascagoula tribe—men, women, and children—joined hands and sang a dirge while they walked into the river and drowned. Since that time, the river has been known to sing. Some say it is from the Pascagoula tribe that still swims beneath the waters.

An 1892 article in the *New Orleans Times-Picayune* says that people came from far and wide to listen to the "flutelike sounds that are rubbed off from the river, as a deft hand brushes melody from the rim of a crystal goblet."

A Catholic missionary from de Soto's time wrote that the local Indians believed there were mermaids in the river that would appear on "the surface of the river, as if the still air had been flapped into a whirlwind by myriads of invisible wings."

River Monsters

While we're still in the river, there are more things than mermaids to worry about in Mississippi's waters. Although sharks are saltwater animals, bull sharks that can grow up to twelve feet long use the shallows of Mississippi's freshwater rivers as nurseries. That's not all. The prehistoric-looking alligator gar, which have been reported to grow up to two hundred pounds in some instances, are babies compared to Mississippi's enormous toothy terrors. According to the Mississippi Department of Wildlife, Fisheries, and Parks, the largest alligator gar caught in Mississippi weighed 327 pounds, and stretched 8 feet, 5.25 inches.

If the alligator gar is prehistoric, the gulf sturgeon is Triassic. Literally. Sturgeon fossils date back to the Triassic period, around 245 to 208 million years ago, and still live worldwide. Gulf sturgeons inhabit fresh water in Mississippi, and make alligator gars look small. Although the US Fish and Wildlife Service said these fish grow to about three hundred to four hundred pounds "maximum," there are legends of these beasts getting up to one thousand pounds. Fortunately for swimmers, neither the sturgeon nor alligator gar is harmful to humans. Or are they?

There's no question with actual alligators. Alligators killed two people in 2015 in the United States. That might not sound like much, but shark attacks only resulted in one death in the US that year. In Mississippi, alligators grow big. In 2014, hunter Scott Berry, age forty-two, killed a record 792-pound, thirteen-feet-and-five-inches-long alligator in Mississippi waters.

Mississippi Mud Man

Whether it's called the Skunk Ape, Swamp Ape, Booger, or Mud Man, this hulking, hairy beast is Mississippi's Bigfoot, and there have been some good sightings, like this one from November 2013 in Vicksburg.

David Childers was taking pictures in an abandoned playground, trying to capture a paranormal occurrence, when something large began to crash through the trees, according to the *Jackson (Mississippi) Clarion-Ledger*. "A creature, I don't know what it was, about six feet tall. And it just bolted off through the woods," Childers told the *Clarion-Ledger*. "It was definitely a shaggy coat to it, like a grayish-brown color. When it made the noise that spooked me, I looked over, and it looked like it stood up and just bolted off."

He's not alone. Not long after, a man working near the old playground discovered a large, unshod footprint about nine inches long and six inches wide. Hair he found near the print was grayish-brown, just like that of Childers's monster. According to the *Clarion-Ledger*, historic evidence of a "wood ape" in the area dates back to 1721.

Pascagoula River Aliens

Whether this was an alien encounter, or something out of the realm of cryptozoology, the reality is that Charles Hickson and Calvin Parker Jr., saw something on October 11, 1973, near Gautier that scared the hell out of them, according to the *New York Daily News*.

The two coworkers were fishing on the Pascagoula River one Thursday night when they saw a blue orb in the sky floating toward them. They watched it until it stopped and hovered above the water about one hundred feet from them. As it crawled closer, a strange noise began to emanate from the orb, then the terror started. A hatch opened on the side, and three creatures emerged.

The monsters were five feet tall with "bullet-shaped heads" and no necks. Their mouths, ears, and noses were nothing but slits. Cones "like carrots" protruded from their heads. Their arms ended in claws. The monsters buzzed at the two men, then lifted them off the ground with their claws, and floated with them into the orb.

After an examination, both men were left on the ground in shock as the orb disappeared into the sky.

CHAPTER 25
MISSOURI

ONCE A TERRITORY OF France, Missouri is dotted with French names that we consistently mispronounce, like the city of Versailles (it's pronounced ver-sales, not ver-sahy). I'm from Missouri and even I have a hard time with this. Missouri is known for jazz, barbecue, cattle, baseball, and outlaw Jesse James. It's a midsize state, and has the eighteenth-densest population. Famous residents include President Harry Truman, journalist Walter Cronkite, actors Don Cheadle and Brad Pitt, musician Chuck Berry, baseball great Yogi Berra, Casey Jones (the railroad guy), General John "Blackjack" Pershing, botanist George Washington Carver, astronomer Edwin Hubble, and authors T.S. Eliot and Mark Twain. Covered by plains, hills, forests, and river bottoms, Missouri is as diverse in its geography as it is in culture. From the arts in Kansas City to the food in St. Louis, and all the rural tractor shows in between, Missouri is home to all types of polite people (this is the Midwest, after all), and to some monsters, like space penguins. We can't forget space penguins.

Space Penguins

The mushroom was out of place. It was also green, metal, and enormous. Farmer Claude Edwards found the metallic mushroom in a field on St. Valentine's Day 1967 and went to investigate. At the base of the structure were a number of creatures, about three feet tall, which resembled green waddling penguins with large, black eyes, according to the *Jefferson City News Tribune*.

Acting like any rational, evolved human, he armed himself with rocks and heaved the Stone Age tools toward the ship.

However, Edwards and his rocks ran into a force field about fifteen feet from the craft that kept him away from the penguins. "The whole thing took over five minutes, maybe ten," Edwards told the press about his encounter with the mushroom. "I have never seen anything like it. It looked like shiny silk or something. Couldn't tell. I was going to tell though if I could have hit it with that rock."

Apparently agitated by Edwards's aggressive behavior, the penguins floated into their mushroom, and took off into the sky.

Momo

Sightings of the Missouri Monster (Momo for short) began near the small town of Louisiana in the mid-1900s, but it wasn't until a spate of encounters in the early 1970s that this seven-foot-tall, hairy biped got national attention.

According to the Missouri Folklore Society, the first major sighting occurred in 1971 when Joan Mills and Mary Ryan were picnicking north of town and smelled something awful. "We were eating lunch," Ryan told the press. "We both wrinkled up our noses at the same time. I never smelled anything as bad in my life." Thinking they'd roused a family of skunks, the young women considered abandoning their picnic. What they saw next made them sure of it. A monster was watching them. "It had hair over the body as if it was an ape," Ryan told the press. "Yet, the face was definitely human. It was more like a hairy human."

The beast lurched from the bushes, and stepped toward the women. They screamed, ran to their car, and locked the doors. As the monster tried to get into the car, the women realized the extent of the danger they were in—Mills's keys were in her purse that sat on their picnic blanket down the hill. Sitting in the car in a panic, Mills accidentally bumped the car horn, and the monster ran off—but not before eating their sandwiches.

The next Momo sighting occurred on July 11, 1972. As eight-year-old Terry Harrison and his five-year-old brother, Walley, played outside their home below Marzolf Hill, the boys felt something wasn't right. Terry looked toward the trees and saw an enormous creature covered in long black hair staring at them. He screamed, and his sister Doris, fifteen, who was inside the house, looked out the window to see something out of a nightmare. "It was … six or seven feet tall, black and hairy. It stood like a man, but it didn't look like one to me," she told newspaper reporters, according to the *St. Louis Riverfront Times*. The creature, which seemed to have no neck, fled from the screaming child, carrying a bloody dog in the crook of a muscular, hairy arm. When their father, Edgar, returned home, the monster was long gone, but he found giant footprints, and strange black hairs stuck to the tree where his children had seen the creature.

The encounters at the Harrison house continued. Three days later during a prayer meeting, the prayer group heard unearthly howls and growls in the darkness, forcing the members to flee in terror.

By now stories of the creature had spread over town. According to the *Riverfront Times*, Louisiana man Pat Howard saw the creature running across the road near the Harrison property. Soon after, Ellis Minor, who lived north of Louisiana, shined a flashlight into the trees surrounding his home after his dog started barking. He saw the monster. "I couldn't see its eyes or face. It had hair down 'bout to its hind parts," Minor told a UPI reporter. "As soon as I threw the light on it, it whirled and took off that-a-way."

Sightings continued, and posses were formed to hunt the creature, but to no avail. The Missouri Monster remains a mystery.

Serpent of Mud Lake

Newspapers in the 1800s were rife with fanciful stories of giants and monsters, such as this creature story from the September 19, 1895, edition of the *Hawarden Independent*, of Hawarden, Iowa, describing a monster in a lake near St. Joseph, Missouri:

Wild Story from Western Missouri
Started by a Fisherman

The serpent in Mud Lake, south of this city, has been seen again, this time by Anderson McCoy, a brother of Policeman McCoy. The serpent has been seen a number of times during the past summer and several times it has been caught in nets by fishermen, but broke through the nets, leaving a hole large enough for a horse to pass through. The fishermen have never been able to land it.

McCoy has a strong boat which he uses to hunt ducks on the lake in the season when they are plentiful there. He was out in this boat a few days ago, when something struck it, and he declares it was knocked ten feet into the air. When the boat came down again McCoy saw the serpent swirling in the water a short distance away. He could not see its size or shape, but saw enough of it to know that it is of huge size. His brother's boats have been struck a number of times, but no injury resulted. The fishermen at the lake are considerably excited about the presence of such a mysterious object in the water. McCoy thinks it is a large fish that got into the lake from the river when the water was high.

The Piasa

According to the book *Hidden Animals: A Field Guide to Batsquatch, Chupacabra, and Other Elusive Creatures* by Michael Newton, in 1857, passengers on a steamboat traveling up the Missouri River saw a "great undulating serpent" in the sky that breathed fire. Other accounts of dragons that stretch back to Native American folklore include the Piasa "bird" described in 1836 by Professor John Russell of Shurtleff College in Upper Alton, Illinois. According to Russell's work "The Tradition of the Piasa," the monster began to attack local Indians after feasting off the spoils of war had given it a taste for human flesh. The dragon was later slain by an Indian warrior.

The Piasa is a winged creature with green scales, horns, and a long tail that is said to either live in the rocky crags above the Mississippi River valley, or in a whirlpool in the river itself.

Giants

Stories of gigantic human skeletons crop up all across North America. One such giant story is from Missouri. On April 9, 1885, the *New York Times* published the article "Missouri's Buried City," that chronicled the discovery of an enormous ancient city in a coalmine underneath the city of Moberly. What thrilled the explorers was the size of the city's former inhabitants.

Here's an excerpt:

> But the curiosity was the skeleton ... Mr. Morehouse, who had a tape line with him measured the bones of the leg. The femur measured four and a half feet, and the tibia four feet and three inches, showing that the creature, when alive, must have been endowed with both muscular power and quick action. The head bones had in two places separated the sagittal and the coronal suturis having been destroyed. The party judged, from the best information to be obtained on so a short time, that the skeleton is about three times as large as that of an average man, but they were afraid to attempt its removal this morning with the poor appliances at hand. Consequently it was left where found, to be removed at the earliest hour that the work can be done.

Unfortunately, that's the last the world heard of the Missouri giants.

The Night People

Young Vern Windsor often saw people outside his house at night. From age five to six, Vern would look out his bedroom window in Orrick to see people with large, fishlike eyes walking around his yard, and sometimes into his neighbors' houses. At the time, this wasn't strange to him. "They were the Night People," Vern said plainly. Everyone Vern knew—himself, his family, his friends—lived in the real world during the day. The people he saw outside his bedroom window lived there when the sun went down. "In my mind we were the Day People and they were the Night People. I know that sounds weird but that's how it seemed."

Vern, now an adult living in nearby Liberty, thought the Night People were normal. "I'd wake up at night and see these people with big eyes living a regular life," he said. "I could see faces, clothes, they had kids...I do remember the adult mowing the yard. But I thought it was weird because I couldn't hear the mower."

He also watched them walk up and down the street, pausing to speak with each other. "They seemed like they were talking and interacting normally," Vern said. "Like down home. You'd just see people talking." When Vern's family moved from Orrick to Liberty, he saw the same fish-eyed Night People outside his window. Then, one night, he finally made contact and never saw them again.

"The children were playing in the yard next door and I thought, hey, I might go play with them," he said. "What's weird, though, is the last time I saw them, it seemed like all of a sudden they seemed to notice that I'd noticed them. One of the adults just looked at me and just realized, 'they see me now.' And the next thing I see is it's daylight and I never see (them) again."

Vern had blacked out, and came to hours later. "If this was real, I probably wasn't perceived as a threat until I decided to come out and play," Vern said.

CHAPTER 26
MONTANA

MONTANA IS BIG. THE kind of big reserved for entire countries. To give a sense of scale, it's roughly the same size as, but still bigger than, Japan, and it's only America's fourth-largest state. In its 147,040 square miles Montana brushes four states and three Canadian provinces. Known as "Big Sky Country," Montana is split by the Continental Divide, and consists of the Great Plains in the east that stretch to the Dakotas, and numerous mountain ranges in the west—the most notable of which is the Rocky Mountains.

The state boasts Yellowstone National Park, Glacier National Park, and Little Bighorn Battlefield National Monument (named for the 1876 battle in which Lakota warriors annihilated a force led by General George Armstrong Custer). Famous residents include daredevil motorcyclist Evel Knievel, *Twin Peaks* creator and director David Lynch, Pearl Jam guitarist Jeff Ament, actors Gary Cooper (*High Noon*) and Dirk Benedict (*Battlestar*

FLATHEAD LAKE MONSTER

Galactica), and the Unabomber Ted Kaczynski. Montana may be enormous, but it's forty-eighth in population density. That's plenty of room for monsters to roam free.

Shunka Warak'in

Most evidence of cryptids involves fuzzy pictures, footprints in plaster, and in some cases blood and hair samples, but with Montana's cryptid the Shunka Warak'in there's actually a body. The mounted creature measures forty-eight inches long, not including the tail, and stands twenty-eight inches tall at the shoulder, according to the *Bozeman (Montana) Daily Chronicle*.

Rancher Israel Ammon Hutchins shot the animal on his property in 1886. Although the beast was unknown to white settlers, the local Native Americans knew what it was, naming it Shunka Warak'in, which means "carries off dogs." According to the book *Trails to Nature's Mysteries: The Life of a Working Naturalist*, written by Ross Hutchins, his grandfather Israel saw the "wolflike beast of dark color was chasing my grandmother's geese." He shot at it, but missed. Others saw the creature. "Those who got a good look at the beast describe it as being nearly black and having high shoulders and a back that sloped downward like a hyena," Hutchins wrote.

One morning, Israel heard his dogs barking in alarm and got another shot at the hyena-like beast. "This time he was able to kill it," Hutchins wrote. "Just what the animal was is still an open question. After being killed, it was donated to a man named (Joseph) Sherwood who kept a combination grocery and museum at Henry Lake in Idaho. It was mounted and displayed there for many years. He called it ringdocus." The mounted creature is now back in the hands of the Hutchins family; Jack Kirby, Israel

Hutchins's grandson, purchased the mounted Shunka Warak'in in 2007.

Although the Shunka Warak'in has not undergone DNA testing (Kirby is resistant to the idea), some have speculated it to be a Borophagus, a hyena-like dog once found in North America. Unfortunately for that theory, the Borophagus existed during the Pleistocene era and has been extinct since the last Ice Age. What the Shunka Warak'in was remains a mystery.

A Hairy, Bear-Eating Monster

Newspapers in the 1800s were a bit more exciting than the newspapers of today. With stories of elections, wars, and Kardashians, today's headlines (even those of monsters) can't compare with headlines of monsters more than one hundred years ago—like the story "A Montana Monster" that appeared in New York's *Brooklyn Eagle* on November 4, 1892.

An unnamed mountain man apparently saw a large, hairy creature with a "habit of rising on its haunches and walking on its hind legs after the manner of a gorilla." The witness claimed this man-like monster killed and ate "several large bears" and "one mountain sheep," after he discovered half-eaten carcasses near what he described as a "headquarters" of the beast. Although this was the only reported sighting of such a monster at the time, the mountains of southern Montana near the Wyoming border would be ripe territory for Bigfoot.

The Flathead Lake Monster

At twenty-eight miles long, sixteen miles wide, and 370 feet deep, Montana's Flathead Lake is the largest natural freshwater lake west of the Mississippi River, and similar in size to Scotland's Loch Ness (larger in surface area, but only half as deep). It also shares something with the loch—the legend of a monster.

The first reported encounter with this creature was by steamboat Captain James C. Kerr in 1889. Kerr and a number of passengers saw what they first thought to be a log, but as the boat got closer, witnesses claimed the object in the water was a whale. Numerous reports of the creature have surface over the decades. Witnesses have said the monster is everything from a giant eel, to a sturgeon, to a forty-foot-long plesiosaur.

A number of sightings occurred in 1993, including large and small humped creatures witnesses thought may be a mother and child in Big Arm Bay. Another account by bankers from Seattle describes a dark, twelve-foot-long, eel-like shape beneath the water.

There have been at least ninety-seven reported sightings of the Flathead Lake Monster over the years, according to a story on KECI, the NBC affiliate in Missoula. Former fisheries biologist Laney Hanzel told the station the sightings are all similar—a dark serpent with black eyes. "[Witnesses] have been doctors, they have been lawyers, very sincere people," Hanzel told KECI. "With the evidence that I've seen, I would say they have been telling me the truth."

Thunderbirds

The Thunderbird is a Native American legend that stretches across North America. It is an enormous bird whose name comes from the thunderous beating of its wings. The Thunderbird closely resembles a family of bird called the Teratorn that existed between the Miocene and Pleistocene periods and had a wingspan that stretched to twenty feet in length. These beasts from another age have been seen in Montana.

According to reports filed with the Montana cryptozoologist Thomas Marcum, a man and his father driving on Interstate 90 witnessed the "largest bird I have ever seen, bigger than an eagle or turkey vulture," the anonymous witness claimed. The report said the bird, which was "shaped like a bird of prey," had a wingspan of fifteen to twenty feet. It was overhead for about fifteen seconds before it flew out of sight.

CHAPTER 27
NEBRASKA

THE STATE OF NEBRASKA sits in the center of North America and is part of the Great Plains. The population of the state is nearly two million people, and it is scattered with small towns. Eighty-nine percent of the towns in Nebraska have populations of fewer than three thousand people, which gives the state the feel of a Norman Rockwell painting. Nebraska is one of the biggest producers of beef and corn in the country. Famous Nebraskans include such diverse personalities as religious leader Malcolm X; comedian Larry the Cable Guy; the fourth-richest man in the world, Warren Buffett; Oscar-winning actor (and Superman's dad) Marlon Brando; and US president Gerald Ford. Although Nebraska is mostly prairieland, it is dotted with a number of lakes, such as the former Alkali Lake (now Walgren Lake), home of the Alkali Lake Monster.

ALKALI LAKE MONSTER

Alkali Lake Monster

Lurking in the depths of this fifty-acre lake in northwest Nebraska is a monster, sightings of which stretch back into Native American legend. The forty- to one-hundred-foot-long creature resembles a giant brown alligator with a rhinoceros horn on its nose—and it smells awful.

According to the Nebraska State Historical Society, the earliest newspaper account of the creature was in a 1922 edition of the nearby *Hay Springs News*. An article the next year in the *Omaha (Nebraska) World Herald* brought more attention to the lake. The *World Herald* article states J.A. Johnson and two friends were camping on the shores of the lake when the creature interrupted their relaxing weekend. Johnson said the monster saw the three men, and thrashed its tail, roared, and dropped under the water. Local residents blamed the monster for animal disappearances in the area.

Although in later years the monster was thought to be a hoax created by newspaperman John G. Maher, the nearby town of Hay Springs isn't giving up on it quite yet. They sell too many T-shirts.

The Loess Man

In 1894, men digging for Native American remains ten miles north of Omaha dug up a skull they couldn't readily identify, so they packed it up and forgot about it. Twelve years later, after a similar skull was found in Nebraska by Robert Fletcher Gilder from the University of Nebraska, they sent the skull to Gilder for comparison. Gilder was certain they had uncovered remains of a Neanderthal.

In the November 16, 1906, issue of *Science Magazine*, Gilder claimed exactly that. "The skulls are of the Neanderthal type," he wrote. "With thick protruding brows, low forehead devoid of frontal eminences, large parietal eminences, narrow temples, thick skull walls, and small brain capacity."

Evidence of Neanderthal in the center of North America would have shattered the accepted theory that only modern humans migrated to that continent across the Bering Strait land bridge twelve thousand to thirteen thousand years ago. Neanderthals—limited to Africa and Eurasia—became extinct forty thousand years ago.

Anthropologist Ales Hrdlicka, in his book *Skeletal Remains Suggesting or Attributed to Early Man in North America* (1907), set out to discredit the Loess Man, claiming since the skulls were discovered only four feet down, they were modern skulls, and couldn't be Neanderthal. However, he couldn't explain the protruding brows, or the low forehead.

Neanderthals in Nebraska? Who knows.

Phantom Kangaroos

In 1958, Grand Island businessman Charles V. Wetzel was fishing on the Platte River about eight miles outside of town when he saw something that shouldn't be. According to a July 28, 1958, Associated Press story, Wetzel thought he saw a deer, until it moved, bounding away on enormous back legs in ten-foot leaps. He'd seen a kangaroo about 8,700 miles away from the beast's home in Australia.

Kangaroos have been seen worldwide in areas without native populations since the 1830s. Sightings stretch across North America, France, the UK, Japan, and Poland. Although in some countries, like Poland, escaped kangaroos have formed colonies, that can't account for all of the sightings of these bounding marsupials that are so far away from home.

Vampire

An article by Dale Bacon, the assistant curator of the Nebraska State Historical Society, claims Nebraska cowboys encountered a vampire in the late 1890s. And with a name like Bacon, I trust him.

In 1895 around Pine Ridge, ranch hands, cattle, and wildlife were reportedly attacked by a madman. Ranch hands witnessed this man chase down cattle, wrestle them to the ground, and rip at the bovine throat with his hands and teeth. The man would then lap "the blood of his victim the way a dog laps water."

A cowboy named Jack Lewis ran into this man people now called a vampire. Alone in the darkness one night, the vampire attacked Lewis. However, Lewis was able to pull his gun and fire two shots. The vampire ran into the night; Lewis and other ranch hands chased him on horseback, but they never found the vampire. Back at camp, the hands tended Lewis's wounds— tooth and claw marks on his face and neck.

Bigfoot

When the discussion of Bigfoot comes around, the first place that comes to mind isn't usually Nebraska. However, there have been plenty of Big Hairy sightings in the Cornhusker State— more than two dozen during a spate in 1977 alone. One sighting north of Lincoln, Nebraska, was as recent as July 2014.

According to an article in the *Lincoln Journal Star*, a fifteen-year-old boy driving a vehicle on a gravel road near the Platte River at about 5:30 a.m. saw a hairy, seven-foot-tall creature walk into the road in front of his vehicle. The beast went on two legs, like a human. After it crossed the road it disappeared into the trees. Later, the boy and a friend returned to the spot and found strange hair stuck to a broken cornstalk.

"It certainly generated a lot of coffee shop conversation," Saunders County Sheriff Kevin Stukenholtz told the *Journal Star*. Although Stukenholtz told the *Omaha World Herald* he doesn't think the boy saw a Bigfoot, he also doesn't think the boy is pulling a hoax.

Apart from this new sighting, Nebraska Game and Parks conservation agent Mike Luben said he's received three calls about Bigfoot in the past twenty-four years. "To be honest with you," he told the *Journal Star*. "It's kind of like a mountain lion call. Most don't turn out to be mountain lions, but you never know."

CHAPTER 28
NEVADA

NEVADA IS A BIG state. Nestled in the American Southwest, Nevada takes up 110,567 square miles (roughly the size of Italy), making it the seventh-largest state in the union. Although known for its deserts (it has ten), Nevada is also a state for mountains, many topping ten thousand feet. The name "Nevada" is derived from the Spanish *nevada*, which means "snowy." Nevada is one of the largest gold producers in the world, and also supplies a fair amount of silver. This state is also known for the forbidden. With legal gambling, legal prostitution, and the mysterious Area 51, you'd think the state of Nevada would have enough going for it without being home to monsters. I guess not.

Tahoe Tessie

Lake Tahoe covers an area of 191.6 square miles (the size of the Micronesian country of Palau) and stretches across the Nevada state line into California. At 1,646 feet deep, it's the world's

TAHOE TESSIE

tenth-deepest lake. The story of a beast dwelling in the lake goes back centuries. The Washoe and Paiute people had a legend of a serpentlike monster that lived in a cave beneath the lake. Sightings of a serpent that stretches up to eighty feet long have continued to modern days.

In 1959, police officer Mickey Daniels and a fellow fisherman were on Lake Tahoe in his forty-three-foot boat when a wake rocked them. However, there were no other boats in the area. "It's not a wake from the boat," Daniels told the *Los Angeles Times*. The wake came from something under the water, then it disappeared.

In 1979, a witness claimed he and three other people watched an enormous serpent hunting a school of trout. "It was about as big around as a telephone pole and maybe thirty to sixty feet in length from what we could see of it," the anonymous source told WeirdCalifornia.com. "It didn't swim like a snake. It was diving up and splashing down with its head [and] neck into the school of fish, which were leaping out of the water ahead of it. We were speechless for several minutes afterward."

Fishermen reported seeing a fifteen-foot-long serpent swim underneath their boat in the 1980s. Numerous witnesses in the 1990s, 2000s, and 2010s have claimed to see the hump and head of an enormous creature in the lake.

Explanations range from a surviving plesiosaur, to a freshwater eel, to a sturgeon.

Jarbidge Monster

The unincorporated town of Jarbidge sits in the 113,167-acre Jarbidge Wilderness in the mountains of Elko County in northeastern Nevada. A thirty-foot-tall giant is said to lurk nearby. The name Jarbidge is a Shoshone Indian word that means "monster that lurks in the canyon." Local legend claims the giant named Tsawhawbitts grabbed anyone who ventured into his canyon, put them into a basket, and carried the victims to his cave where he'd eat them. The Shoshone chased Tsawhawbitts into the cave, and imprisoned this man-eating monster by blocking the entrance with boulders.

Pterosaur

Two men from California were driving near Winnemucca, Nevada, in June 2015 when they encountered a gray, leathery "bird" on Interstate 80, according to the website Cryptozoology News. Their headlights shone on the creature at about 11:00 p.m. It had a long, thin neck, a long beak, and a head crest. There were claws on the end of its seven-foot-wide bat-like wings. The creature struggled to get airborne, and barely cleared the top of the man's car. The driver identified it as a pterosaur.

Although thought to have been extinct for sixty-five million years, sightings of living pterosaurs have been reported across the world, including Arkansas, Kansas, and Texas.

Lovelock Skull

In 1967, an ancient skull was found near Lovelock Cave that resembled that of a Neanderthal. The skull had a protruding brow ridge, sloping forehead, and a large occipital bun—all traits rare in modern humans, although not unheard of. It did not resemble the skull of Native Americans. Local Paiute Indians had a legend of red-haired barbarians who killed the Paiute for food. The Paiute hunted down this tribe of barbarians and exterminated it.

Much like the Loess Man skull discovered near Omaha, Neanderthal remains in North America are considered impossible by mainstream science. Neanderthals—limited to Africa and Eurasia—became extinct forty thousand years ago.

Gargantuan Gliders

In 1925, a pilot named Don Wood Jr. encountered something in the Nevada desert he couldn't explain. Although he kept silent about it for thirty-four years for fear of ridicule, in 1959 he wrote a letter to the magazine *Flying Saucers* to explain what he saw.

Wood landed his two-seat airplane on a mesa near Battle Mountain early one afternoon. While exploring the top of the mesa, Wood and his companion saw something about eight feet wide attempting to land. It was round and flat with a red belly. It stopped, and when Wood and his friend approached it, they discovered it was alive. "It was hurt," he wrote in the letter. "And as it breathed the top would rise and fall, making a half-foot hole all around it like a clam opening and closing."

After observing the creature for about twenty minutes, it began to pulsate. "So help me the thing grew as bright as all get out," Wood wrote. "Except where it was hurt."

Suddenly a shadow covered the men, and they looked to find a similar thirty-foot-wide creature descending onto the mesa. It grabbed the smaller monster with "four sucker-like tongues" and took off into the air, disappearing with incredible speed.

CHAPTER 29
NEW HAMPSHIRE

COMPARED TO MOST OF the United States, New Hampshire is small. The Dominican Republic—which shares a Caribbean island with another country—is twice the size of New Hampshire. Yes, New Hampshire is small, but what it lacks in size it makes up for in beauty. Forests of white pine, red oak, northern hardwood, and birch stretch over great swaths of the state, along with lakes—944 of them (natural and man-made), the biggest of which is the 44,586-acre Lake Winnipesaukee. And mountain ranges, sixteen of them with forty-eight peaks taller than four thousand feet. New Hampshire is known for winter sports, for being the first colony to form a government independent of England, and for being the birthplace of people who changed the world, by which I mean the McDonald brothers—founders of McDonald's Restaurant. Oh, sure, President Franklin Pierce was from New Hampshire, as was astronaut Alan Shepard, and rocker Ronnie James Dio. Then there are the Devil Monkeys.

WOOD DEVIL

Devil Monkeys

Something hairy lurks in the New Hampshire area of the Appalachian Mountains. Monkeys reported anywhere from three feet to eight feet long have been seen in the mountains, and more recently in towns. These primates, with doglike muzzles, have long black hair streaked with white, pointed ears, and a nasty temper. Devil Monkeys have been known to kill pets and livestock.

Sightings of Devil Monkeys go back to the 1950s, when a baboon-like monster attacked a couple's car. The most recent report came from 2001 in the small town of Danville, population of just over four thousand. A group of twelve people encountered an enormous, hooting monkey inside the city limits. "It wasn't a sound I had heard before," a witness said.

What is the New Hampshire Devil Monkey? An escaped pet? A North American primate? A spirit? Until one is captured, the residents of New Hampshire will never know.

Wood Devils

There seem to be a lot of devils in New Hampshire.

These tall, thin, gray-haired, bipedal monsters live deep in the forests. These creatures are alert for intruders in their territory, so witnesses tend to only see them by accident. Wood Devils are adept at hiding, standing still against a tree, and blending in with the bark. When spooked, Wood Devils can run at great speed.

An account from 1991 near the Androscoggin River paints the Wood Devil as elusive and silent. The witness, walking through the trees, heard twigs snap behind him. When he turned, nothing was there. However, looking closer, he saw a tall, thin, gray figure move away from a tree, then vanish behind another. The creature was about seven feet tall and covered in hair.

Although people now consider New Hampshire's Wood Devil sightings to be of Bigfoot, the slight build and slinking behavior make this unlikely.

Dublin Lake Monster

Dublin Lake, sometimes called Dublin Pond, is a 240-acre, sixty-four-foot-deep body of water in southwestern New Hampshire, and it has a less than savory reputation. According to the book *America's Loch Ness Monsters* by Philip Rife, Dublin Lake has resident creepy-crawlies that lurk in its underwater caverns.

In the 1980s, a scuba diver apparently ventured deep into Dublin Lake, and disappeared. He was found naked days later, unconscious amongst the trees along the shore. When revived, he mumbled about eel-like monsters he'd encountered under the cold waters of the lake. A similar story about Dublin Lake involves a diver encountering a dry pocket in an underground cavern and witnessing some sort of cryptid.

Although the tale of Dublin Lake monsters has taken on a fanciful status, you never know what hides under the cold, dark waters of America's lakes.

Pukwudgie

The Wampanoag Indians of New England told tales of gray, child-sized trolls with big ears and noses, that could use magic, such as disappearing, morphing into a walking porcupine, and create fire by thought.

Never make one angry.

According to the legends of the Wampanoag, the Pukwud-gie became angry at the affection the Wampanoag showed the legendary giant Maushop. The Pukwudgie played tricks on Wampanoag Indians, stole their children, and burned their villages. Jerks. The Pukwudgie are also known to lure unsuspecting hikers to their death, or, if they're feeling particularly spunky, they simply shoot people with poison arrows.

Pukwudgie encounters are still reported to this day. Small humanlike creatures pester lone hikers and bicyclists, and attempt (and succeed?) to push people from cliffs.

CHAPTER 30
NEW JERSEY

FOR ITS SIZE, THE Garden State has people—lots and lots of people. New Jersey can brag about having the highest population density in the United States at 1,030 people per square mile; the national average is 91.5. It is home to the oldest seashore resort in the country (Cape May), a bevy of diners (New Jersey is called the Diner Capital of the World), and it is the place of inventions. Thomas Edison invented the phonograph, the motion picture projector, and the light bulb at his lab in Menlo Park. The motion picture projector also plays into another bit of New Jersey history: the state offered the first drive-in movie theater. New Jersey has 130 miles of ocean coastline, and is the launching spot for ferries that take visitors to the Statue of Liberty—also in New Jersey. Famous people from New Jersey include Apollo astronaut Buzz Aldrin; basketball greats Shaquille O'Neal and Dennis Rodman; *Game of Thrones* author George R.R. Martin and *Game of Thrones* actor Peter Dinklage; musicians Count Basie, Frank Sinatra, Bruce Springsteen, and Whitney Houston;

JERSEY DEVIL

actors Abbott and Costello (yes, both of them), Jerry Lewis, and Jack Nicholson; and magician David Copperfield. And that's the short list. Then there's that little pesky thing called the Jersey Devil.

The Jersey Devil

The Pine Barrens of New Jersey. The name is simply ominous. That area is called the Barrens because this coastal plain of pine forest that juts from sandy, acidic soil is barren of any plant life humans can survive on. The Barrens is home to a wide variety of plants, like orchids, vines, and the carnivorous pitcher plants bladderwort and sundew. The Pine Barrens slogan is, "A place so dangerous even the plants will eat you."

Dead communities dot the Barrens, some with crumbling buildings, others with brick foundations peeking from amongst the foliage (foliage that wants you dead). The people who once tried to conquer the Pine Barrens are long gone. It's the most rural spot in New Jersey, and home to the state's greatest legend.

The legend of the Devil goes something like this—No. Wait. It goes exactly like this.

In 1735, a pregnant woman named Mother Leeds cursed her soon-to-be born thirteenth child as a "devil." Legend has it the baby was born looking like any other child, but almost immediately its head stretched into the semblance of a goat, its hands and feet turned to hooves, bat-like wings sprang from its sides, and a barbed tail grew as the horrified parents watched. The newly born monster slaughtered the midwife that had just helped it into this world, and disappeared up the chimney.

Plenty of people have reported seeing the Devil during the past 280 years, including Joseph Bonaparte (yep, Napoleon's brother), and plenty of farmers with dead livestock. Unidentified noises and strange animal tracks have kept the Devil's legacy alive.

The biggest week for the Jersey Devil was in January 1909 when it appeared throughout the state, and into neighboring Pennsylvania. A strange, bat-winged creature attacked a trolley car in Haddon Heights, New Jersey. In Bristol, Pennsylvania (just across the Delaware River), police officers attempted to shoot a monster that fit the description of the Jersey Devil, although the policemen either missed the Devil, or the bullets had no effect. More sightings of the Devil across New Jersey caused widespread panic. Schools closed, and men stayed home from work.

Although over the years people have tried to prove the Jersey Devil a hoax, the winged, demonic spawn of Mother Leeds continues to be a staple in New Jersey folklore.

Wemategunis

The Lenape (also known as the Delaware Indians) tell of the Wemategunis, the little people of their mythology. These dwarves are about three feet tall and much like little people legends from around the globe, you don't want to make them angry. Although usually benevolent, if upset the Wemategunis will use their unnatural strength and ability to become invisible to prank unsuspecting people, sometimes painfully.

One legend tells of a hunter who experienced the Wemategunis after he wandered off from his group. The lost hunter killed a deer and, while he was looking for his companions, a mocking voice called to him. The hunter crisscrossed a valley, trying to find the person calling to him, but the voice was just beyond his search. He finally threw the deer down in anger, and rushed toward the voice. He came face-to-face with a Wemate-gunis, who laughed and said he only called because he wanted to see how long the hunter could run carrying the deer.

Not cool, man.

Big Red Eye

Back in the 1970s, residents of the mountainous, wooded area of northwest New Jersey became aware of something strange in the forest. Something big, something hairy, something loud.

According to a report by CBS2 in New York, this beast has a reputation. "It comes out at nighttime with big red eyes," Alex Zenerovitz of Newtown told CBS2.

People call it Big Red Eye.

Witnesses claim this creature—the New Jersey Bigfoot—is well over six feet tall, weighs about four hundred pounds, and can emit a scream that will freeze your blood. In the CBS2 report, Tom Card, a retired forest ranger, said he heard the shriek while in the woods more than forty years ago. The scream sent him and two other rangers—both armed—running from the trees.

"It was a wailing, howling kind of a scream," Card said in the report. "They were a little unnerved because they had never heard anything like this either."

Neither Card nor the other two rangers returned to that section of the forest.

Can Bigfoot be hiding in New Jersey? With more than two million acres of forestland, you betcha.

The White Stag

Although the Pine Barrens have the reputation of being dangerous, not all stories of strange creatures lurking there are wicked.

In the days when people relied on horses for transportation, a stagecoach traveling through the Pine Barrens near dusk was caught up in a rainstorm. The driver, making his way toward a tavern on the other side of the well-used Quaker Bridge, pulled the stage to a stop, which didn't help the mood of his already tired and frustrated passengers. The coach driver stopped because an enormous white stag blocked the way.

The stagecoach horses, frightened to almost the point of panic, were nearly too much for the driver to handle, and he grabbed his rifle to be rid of the deer. When the driver's feet hit the muddy road, and he approached the deer, it turned and disappeared into trees.

At closer inspection of where the deer stood, the driver discovered it had blocked the coach's passage onto the bridge—which had been washed away by the swollen river.

To this day, if a hunter sees a white stag in the Barrens, he lets it be.

CHAPTER 31
NEW MEXICO

MOUNTAINS AND DESERT MAKE up much of the state of New Mexico. Bordered by Texas, Arizona, Colorado, (not enough of Oklahoma to really count), and Mexico, the forty-seventh state to join the Union is a mix of rugged Southwest history and a rich art community. The state capital, Santa Fe, was founded by Spanish conquistador Don Pedro de Peralta in 1610. Roughly 2.086 million people call New Mexico home, which is about the population of the nation of Slovenia. In size, New Mexico is 121,589 square miles—Slovenia is 7,780. Yeah, New Mexico is pretty spread out.

Although 64 percent of New Mexico's population speaks English, given its Spanish heritage nearly 30 percent speaks Spanish. Three-and-a-half percent of the population speaks Navajo. Famous people born in New Mexico include animator William Hanna (of Hanna-Barbera), car racing greats Al and Bobby Unser, actor Neil Patrick Harris, and singer John Denver. Dangerous

TERATORN

animals abound in New Mexico, including black bears, jaguars, mountain lions, coyotes, Mexican gray wolves, rattlesnakes, and apparently ridiculously enormous turtles.

Weird Legends of Bottomless Lakes

Bottomless Lakes was the first state park in New Mexico, declared such in 1933, fourteen years before a pesky UFO may (or may not) have crashed at nearby Roswell. The history of Bottomless Lakes stretches back to Spanish conquistadors in the late 1500s searching for the legendary Seven Cities of Gold. Although the Spanish didn't keep record of the lakes, the local Native Americans kept a record of the Spanish, carving a petroglyph at the lakes of one Spanish conquistador riding a horse, according to the article "Legends and Lore of Bottomless Lakes," by John LeMay that appeared in the Roswell, New Mexico, *Centennial* magazine. The lakes (nine in all) got the name "bottomless" by an unlikely source. Legend has it outlaw Billy the Kid and his gang were hiding out at the lakes, and the boys dipped ropes in one lake to see how deep it was. A current kept the ropes from hitting bottom, so the outlaws determined the lakes to be bottomless. The deepest part of any of the nine lakes is 90 feet.

But history isn't the only thing the Bottomless Lakes have to offer. There are the turtles (no, not the late 1960s "Happy Together" American rock band), an octopus man, a white ghost horse, and a dragon. The nine Bottomless Lakes have gained a deadly reputation, swallowing sheep and horses, and in modern days, cars. People drowning in the muddy depths are said to be either victims of a mystical force that transports them to nearby Carlsbad Caverns, or of the turtles.

These reptiles the size of cars are the most popular legend of the murky depth denizens. A boater claimed to see a giant turtle surface in the 1980s; its enormous brown shell made him think Nessie was coming to eat him.

Giants

Enormous human skeletons have been discovered all over the country. New Mexico is no exception. In 1902 the *New York Times* printed the story of ancient giant human skeletons discovered in Guadalupe, New Mexico. This sent "antiquarians and archaeologists" on an expedition to learn more about these enormous peoples due to "the excitement that exists … where an old burial ground has been discovered that has yielded skeletons of enormous size," according to the article.

A rancher named Luiciana Quintana apparently discovered an ancient burial site with graves holding skeletons at least twelve feet tall. "The men who opened the grave say the forearm was four feet long and that in a well-preserved jaw the lower teeth ranged from the size of a hickory nut to that of the largest walnut in size," according to the *Times*. "The chest of the being is reported as having a circumference of seven feet."

Unfortunately, much like similar discoveries of the time, the fate of the skeletons, as well as the scientific investigation, are lost in the annals of history.

Teratorns

People have reported encountering enormous birds across the United States—birds that, by the descriptions, went extinct around twelve thousand years ago. New Mexico is no different. A long-time resident of the Doña Ana Mountains told KRQE

News in 2007 that he saw something in 1998 he still couldn't believe.

One day while hiking, Dave Zander saw two giant birds perched on a rocky crag nearly a mile away. "These creatures were so huge they looked like the size of small planes," Zander told KRQE. "All of the sudden one of them…dropped off the top of the mountain, came down the front of the mountain and all the sudden these huge wings just spread out."

Zander estimated the wingspan at twenty feet. "Not a normal bird. Definitely of a giant variety," he said. "It makes you feel like it could come over and carry you off if it wanted to." The closest animal that would fit Zander's description is the Teratorn, which became extinct during the Pleistocene era.

New Mexico isn't immune to supposedly extinct creatures in its skies. A Colorado man reportedly witnessed a pterosaur in northeast New Mexico in the early 1970s, and in the 1800s residents of Lordsburg, New Mexico, claimed to see giant featherless birds often.

Spring-Heeled Jack

What?

Spring-Heeled Jack was a humanlike entity seen across Great Britain in the 1800s. What the hell's he doing in New Mexico? I'll get to that.

Although Jack terrorized parts of Scotland, he mostly lurked around the streets of London. Witnesses described him as a tall, thin man who wore a helmet, tight white clothing, and a black cape. He had razor claws, blazing red eyes, and could breathe blue fire. Sounds like he could have been in the X-Men. And he was apparently quite pleased with himself. This shrieking, giggling monster would pounce in front of coaches, terrifying the horses and sending the coach and startled coachman flying off into the night. Jack would then pounce away, sometimes effortlessly leaping over nine-foot-tall fences.

Although Jack didn't kill anyone, he was credited with causing sudden cases of madness among young women.

Although by 1938 Spring-Heeled Jack encounters had all but stopped in Great Britain, young people in Silver City, New Mexico (who claimed to have never heard of Spring-Heeled Jack), reported encounters with a red-eyed, jumping, giggling man in a cape.

CHAPTER 32
NEW YORK

THE STATE OF NEW York is slightly bigger than the country of Nicaragua, with a population of 19.8 million—8.55 million of that in New York City alone (Nicaragua's population is 6.08 million). With a gross domestic product nearly the same as Mexico, New York is vital to the economy of the United States. The first Europeans to walk New York soil were French and Dutch colonists. The French eventually migrated northward and settled in Quebec. When the British annexed the region from the Dutch, they named the new British colony New York, after the Duke of York. Bordered by Canada, five states, and the Atlantic Ocean, New York has more than 18.9 million acres of forestland, and 7,600 freshwater lakes. Famous residents include basketball great (and *Space Jam* star) Michael Jordan; President Donald Trump; actors Robert Downy Jr., Tom Cruise, Sylvester Stallone (the list goes on); and musicians the Ramones, Tupac

EAST RIVER MONSTER

Shakur, the Beastie Boys, the Velvet Underground, and KISS. Although New York is home to lots and lots of water monsters, let's start with Wildmen, and a giant.

Wildmen

Large, hairy, manlike creatures have been reported by settlers of New York since 1818. According to *Voices: The Journal of New York Folklore*, the first reported encounter with a Wildman was outside the town of Ellisburg near the Canadian border. A "gentleman of unquestionable veracity" saw a hairy, stooped man running through the woods. The townsfolk turned out to hunt for the Wildman, but he remained elusive.

Other reports were sporadic. A young hunter told his father he had a run-in with a hairy boy in August 1838 near the border town of Silver Lake, Pennsylvania. Told to shoot anything that wasn't a person or domesticated animal, he was on alert when he heard someone coming toward him in the woods. Readying himself, he saw a six- or seven-year-old boy covered in black hair. The boy stopped about thirty feet from him, and stared at him. Terrified, the young hunter shot at the boy, but his hands were shaking so hard he missed the creature that turned and fled into the trees.

In 1869, a group of nearly one hundred people saw a Wildman in Steuben County. The hairy monster screamed as it ran "with a springing, jerking hitch in his gait [which] gave him more the appearance of a wild animal than a human being," according to the *Plattsburgh Sentinel*. One witness told the *Evening Gazette* the Wildman had "long, matted hair; the thick, black, uncombed beard; the wild, glaring, bloodshot eyeballs, which seemed bursting from their sockets; the swage, haggard, unearthly countenance;

the wild, beastly appearance of this thing, whether man or animal, has haunted me."

A horseman saw a Wildman in July 1895 near Margaretville, New York. A "wild-eyed man or ape" with "long and hairy arms" stood in the road ahead, according to *Voices*. The monster—at least seven feet tall—screamed, and grabbed one of the man's horses, dragging it into the darkness at the side of the road. A farmer shot at the apelike creature, but the beast threw him to the ground and ran off.

Hundreds of such sightings sprinkle the annals of the state's history. Throughout the 1970s and 1980s, the Kinderhook area has had enough sightings of this Bigfoot-like monster it's been called the "Kinderhook Creature."

Cardiff Giant

On October 16, 1869, well diggers near Cardiff uncovered a ten-foot, four-and-a-half-inch petrified man. The stone man was then, of course, put on display for twenty-five cents a peek. The giant quickly became such a popular attraction for farmer William Newell that he hiked the price to fifty cents.

However, there was something odd about the giant. Archaeologists and geologists called the giant a fraud, although the religious community supported the idea of a giant because of giants in the Bible. None of this mattered to people in the area, who still lined up to see the giant. Circus showman P.T. Barnum offered $50,000 for the giant, and when his offer was turned down, he had his own giant made.

In an 1870 court case, New York tobacconist George Hull admitted creating the giant and planting it to be discovered by the well diggers. The giant, which has been featured in everything from a Mark Twain short story to a 2012 indie rock album, is on display in the Farmers' Museum in Cooperstown, New York.

East River Monster

In July 2012, photographer Denise Ginley and her boyfriend took a walk along the East River toward a farmer's market, when they discovered a rotting monster. "We were horrified by it and we took some camera phone pictures and then finally we decided to come back with my camera and I got up the courage to climb over the fence and get closer to it," Ginley told the *New York Daily News*.

Although the New York Parks Department claimed the creature was a "discarded cooked pig," the long, straight tail, and clawed feet make this impossible.

"The Parks Department was probably very quick to identify it as a pig and dispose of it, but it is most certainly not a pig," Ginley told the *Daily News*. "The most obvious sign being the lack of a cloven hoof, instead this creature has five digits all close together."

But what is it? Dr. Paul Curtis, a Cornell University professor, told the *Daily News* it could be a dog, but because of its lack of hair, and decayed state, it was hard to tell.

This sighting is the second such creature in New York. In 2008, a bloated, unidentifiable carcass washed ashore at Montauk, an area of the state steeped in UFO and time travel lore.

Champ

Champlain is a 490-square-mile, four-hundred-foot-deep freshwater lake that lies mostly in New York but also touches Canada and Vermont. It is home to America's most famous lake monster—Champ. The local Native Americans, the Abenaki and the Iroquois, had stories of the monster Tatoskok, a horned serpent that lived under the lake. The first European to see the monster is disputed, although the popular story is that Samuel de Champlain saw something big in the water. But Champlain's sighting was of something less than ten feet long. That's a snack for the next major sighting.

In July 1819, Captain Crum of the ship *Bulwagga Bay* saw a black monster that stretched 187 feet long, according to the *Plattsburgh Republican*. The monster had a head like a sea horse, which stuck about fifteen feet from the water. It had eyes the color of a peeled onion, three teeth, and a white star on its forehead.

A railroad crew saw a gigantic serpent with silvery scales in the lake in 1873. A county sheriff saw a thirty-foot-long "water serpent" in the lake that July, and in August, a steamship collided with a water monster and almost overturned.

Sightings of Champ continue to this day. The most famous photograph of the beast was taken in 1977 and shows a creature with a small head, a long neck, and a hump, which suspiciously resembles the Loch Ness Monster.

Old Greeny

Cayuga Lake, one of upstate New York's glacial finger lakes, has a surface area of 66.41 square miles, is 435 feet deep, and is home to two water monsters. Reports of the monsters date back to the early 1800s, but the first newspaper account didn't appear until 1897 in the *Ithaca Journal*, simply stating that locals were afraid to get too close to the water. In 1929, vacationers reported seeing two creatures about fifteen feet long frolicking in the lake.

Encounters began to get ugly in the 1970s when a toothy eel attacked swimmer Steven Griffen, biting his arm and breaking it. Sightings of Old Greeny are sporadic at best, but continue. Locals think the monster is most probably a sturgeon.

Seneca Lake Monster

Another of the finger lakes, thirty-eight-mile-long, 617-feet-deep Seneca Lake is also the swimming ground of a monster. Local Native American tribes claimed the lake was bottomless, and inhabited by a temperamental creature. European settlers dismissed these stories as fanciful until 1899. According to a 1900 article in the *Seneca Daily News*, steamboat captain Carleton C. Herendeen and his pilot Frederick Rose saw an overturned boat about twenty-five feet long. However, as they closed in on the boat, it turned and swam away. Witnesses aboard the boat saw the monster raise its head and show two rows "of sharp, white teeth." The boat struck the monster, and the impact tossed passengers to the deck.

Sightings continue, although none as exciting as Captain Herendeen's.

Kipsy

Witness reports of a water monster that inhabits the Hudson River between Manhattan and Poughkeepsie vary wildly. Some witnesses say they saw a shark, others a manatee, and still others a sea serpent, according to a 1989 article in the *New York Times*. Most sightings of Kipsy are only humps in the river, but people insist they saw something large and unknown.

CHAPTER 33
NORTH CAROLINA

NORTH CAROLINA IS OF average size when compared to the rest of the forty-nine United States (twenty-eighth out of fifty, still twice as big as Ireland), but it's crowded, ranking ninth in population density with 9.944 million residents. It's home to the highest point in North America east of the Mississippi River (Mount Mitchell at an elevation of 6,684 feet), and more than three hundred miles of coastland. Along with the Atlantic Ocean, and mountains, North Carolina boasts approximately 18.7 million acres of timberland. Famous residents include seventh president Andrew Jackson; NASCAR legend Dale Earnhardt Sr. (and Junior, a NASCAR legend in his own right); Pepsi inventor Caleb Bradham; actors Ava Gardner, Andy Griffith, and Zach Galifanakis; authors O. Henry and Thomas Wolfe; Grammy winner Roberta Flack; boxer Sugar Ray Leonard; and Virginia Dare, the first child born to English parents in North America. Now, let's include some creepy-crawlies with that.

BEAST OF BLADENBORO

Normie

Lake Norman is a man-made lake, the result of the construction of the Cowans Ford Dam between 1959 and 1964—but that doesn't mean it can't have the legend of a monster. With a surface area of around 32,500 acres, and a depth of 130 feet at the south end (although it only averages thirty feet), there's plenty of room for one.

The first report of Normie, the Lake Norman Monster, was in 2002, although the lake had been the source of suspicious wildlife for a while. In the 1990s, freshwater jellyfish inexplicably appeared in Lake Norman. In 2000, it was alligators. Neither species should have been in that lake. So why not a monster?

Witnesses describe Normie as everything from a crocodile (which makes sense due to the alligators), to an enormous fish, to a plesiosaur. On the official Lake Norman Monster website (www.lakenormanmonster.com), a man posted the following encounter:

"I was tubing and I had just fallen off from a quick turn. I floated in the water waiting for the boat and as I did I saw a large neck emerge from the water about five feet in the air. I was terrified because it was only about forty meters from me and I don't know if this thing is mean or not. I quickly turned and started swimming toward the boat as my dad sped toward me because he saw it too. When I got on the boat he said it disappeared right after I turned around."

Although there have been reports for decades of car-sized fish deep in the lake—similar to mostly unsubstantiated reports from most man-made lakes across the country—at least fifty people have claimed seeing Normie in the past few decades.

The Beast of Bladenboro

In the early 1950s, the area around Bladenboro was terrorized by the sudden appearance of a large cat residents blamed for animal mutilations that involved livestock and pets with their jaws either broken or removed. The people of Bladenboro set out to hunt the beast, but it had vanished as quickly as it had come. Fifty years later, the attacks returned with the same style of mutilations.

The first encounter was December 29, 1953, when a resident of Clarkton (eight and a half miles from Bladenboro) went outside to investigate why her neighbor's dogs were barking. What she found was the Beast, a large cat that melted into the night. Two days later, the Beast appeared again, this time near Bladenboro where two farm dogs had been sucked dry of blood.

More attacks followed. The owner of a local gas station watched a large, catlike creature attack a dog, and drag it into the trees. People blamed the increasing animal attacks on a panther, or a bear—then the Beast attacked a local woman. When a local resident went outside to check on yelping dogs, a dark creature the size of a cougar lunged at her. Her screams frightened the Beast, and it bolted away.

Although farmers soon after killed a large bobcat, and deemed it the Beast of Bladenboro, many people doubted that claim. The attacks stopped nonetheless—until 2003. Since then more animals have been reported killed and drained of blood around the Bladenboro area, the largest being three horses.

Whatever the Beast of Bladenboro may be, one thing is certain—it's big.

Demon Dog of Valle Crucis

Valle Crucis (Latin for Valley of the Cross) is a tiny unincorporated community in the Appalachian Mountains. Once the location of a general store that served as a way station between
civilization and the wilderness, today it is a cultural destination
with a calendar filled with music and festivals. It's also home to
legend.

St. John's Episcopal Church, built in the 1860s, sits near the
edge of the small community, and although it is usually as quiet
the rest of the area, its graveyard is the territory of a hellhound.
As the story goes, two students of a nearby college were driving
past the church in the dark when a black hulking shape leapt
from behind a tombstone at the church, and jumped into the
road. The driver slammed on his brakes, and came to rest on
the shoulder of the rural highway. In front of the students was a
snarling black dog the size of a man—it had blazing red eyes.

When the hell beast growled and began to pad toward the
car, the terrified driver took his foot off the brake and stomped
on the accelerator, tearing down the curvy highway at high
speed. The dog not only followed, it closed on the car. However, once the car crossed a bridge the dog stopped chasing them
and melted into the darkness.

The Moon-Eyed People

The ruins of ancient stone monuments dot the Appalachian
Mountains, and according to Native American legends, these are
buildings left by the Moon-Eyed People.

The Moon-Eyed People were a diminutive nocturnal race of men with pale white skin and long beards. They were unable to see in daylight. An 850-foot-long stone wall at the border of North Carolina and Georgia, built between approximately 400 to 500 CE, is credited to the Moon-Eyed People. The wall, anywhere from two to six feet tall, is said to be from a war the Moon-Eyed people fought against the Creek Indians who attacked during the full moon. Even the light of the full moon was too bright for the small bearded people, and the Creek drove the Moon-Eyed People underground, where they are said to remain.

Some attribute the white-bearded Moon-Eyed People to another legend of Welsh travelers led by Prince Madoc, who arrived in that general area of North America in 1170 CE. However, the evidence of a Welsh incursion into North America three hundred years before the arrival of Columbus is tenuous at best. And it's probably safe to say the Welsh have always been able to see in sunlight. The Moon-Eyed People remain a mystery.

CHAPTER 34
NORTH DAKOTA

LOCATED IN THE GREAT Plains of the American Midwest, North Dakota is flat. Really, really flat. At least most of it. The western part of the state (the nineteenth largest of the United States) is dotted with hills and buttes. North Dakota is sparsely populated, with 739,482 residents. The largest city, Fargo, has 113,658 people, which is 15 percent of the entire state's population. North Dakota is bordered by South Dakota, Montana, Minnesota, and the Canadian provinces Manitoba and Saskatchewan. The state experienced an oil boom when the Parshall Oil Field was discovered in 2006, although oil prices are flighty things, and the boom has calmed a bit. Famous North Dakotans include New York Yankees great Roger Maris, astronaut James F. Buchli, 1960s pop singer Bobby Vee, and author Chuck Klosterman. American bison, moose, elk, white pelicans, and eagles are native to the state, and if legends are to be believed, so is the Devils Lake Monster.

MINIWASHITU

Devils Lake Monster

This 330.2-square-mile lake in northeastern North Dakota is host to anglers fishing for perch, walleye, and northern pike. Although not much disturbs the surface of the lake but recreational boats, back when the area was new to European influence, a monster would occasionally poke its head above the water.

The local Native Americans told the settlers stories of a great snake that lived beneath that lake, a serpent that instilled fear in those who saw it. According to a 1915 article in the *Grand Forks Daily Herald*, two well-known businessmen, a police captain, and the pastor of the local Methodist Episcopal Church saw the Devils Lake Monster on different days, and at different points on the lake. Each gave a similar description. The creature was about two feet round, and about sixty feet long.

Unfortunately, the Devils Lake Monster doesn't rear its head above the surface often.

The Miniwashitu

A legend surrounds Little Missouri River, a 560-mile-long tributary of the 2,341-mile-long Missouri River. The legend of the river monster the Miniwashitu. Although sightings of the Miniwashitu are slim, in 1921, curator for the North Dakota State Historical Society Melvin Randolph Gilmore told of one sighting.

In the late 1800s, a man wandering near the river saw an enormous creature rise from the water. Red hair, thick "like a buffalo," covered the beast. The monster had only one eye, and a single horn thrust from its forehead. Its backbone protruded, nocked like "an enormous saw." Terrified, the man made it home before he passed out and later died.

When white settlers spoke of the encounter, local Native Americans told them their fear of the monster. Whoever saw the beast went mad, and usually blind, before succumbing to an untimely death.

Bigfoot

If there were a place for this big furry fellow to hang out, a state as thinly populated as North Dakota would be it. According to an article in the *Aberdeen American News*, there was a rash of Bigfoot reports from the Fort Berthold Indian Reservation when several residents claimed to have seen the elusive creature.

A representative of the Three Affiliated Tribes said tribal officials took photographs of large, humanlike tracks, but wouldn't go so far as to say they were from Bigfoot.

These weren't the first sightings of the creature in North Dakota. A man hunting said a "great ape" stalked him outside his mobile home in Minot. A newspaper clipping from 1908 also chronicles an encounter with Bigfoot.

According to an article from the *Stevens Point Journal*, two cattlemen from Velva, North Dakota, encountered a Wildman outside town. While hunting, the men came face-to-face with the Wildman who had just emerged from the bushes. One of the cattlemen lassoed the Wildman, tied him, loaded him on a horse, and took him to town.

The Wildman was "extremely hairy" with a "grotesque and wild appearance." The man's eyeteeth were "unnaturally elongated in the form of tusks." He would not speak, nor eat, although he drank water from a bucket. There is no report of whatever happened to the hairy Wildman.

Thunderbird

Native American stories of these flying terrors across North America are similar. Thunderbirds can create storms, shoot lightning bolts, and have been known to eat pets—and children.

According to a report from About Paranormal, an Air Force security member in North Dakota stopped to have a smoke in 2009 when he saw what he at first thought was a hang glider drifting across the starry sky. When he grabbed his night vision gear, he realized the glider was a bird with a wingspan of about twenty feet. It flapped its wings and drifted out of sight. Not surprisingly, he never reported his sighting to the Air Force.

CHAPTER 35
OHIO

OHIO, NAMED AFTER THE Iroquois word *ohi-yo* meaning "large creek," lies in the midwestern United States. It's home to a number of firsts, such as America's first automobile (built by John Lambert in 1891), the first use of X-rays in surgery in 1896, Superman (by Jerry Siegel and Joe Shuster in 1933), and the invention of the pop-top can in the 1960s. Eight presidents were either born in Ohio or lived there when they were elected. Along with presidents, Ohio produced movie directors Steven Spielberg and Wes Craven, first man on the moon Neil Armstrong, inventor Thomas Edison, author Toni Morrison, actors Clark Gable and Jim "Thurston Howell III" Backus, and murderer Charles Manson (who also wrote the first draft of the Beach Boys song "Never Learn Not to Love"). Ohio isn't a big state, the thirty-fourth largest, but it ranks seventh in population. Rolling plains make up most of Ohio, topped off by the Appalachian Plateau consisting of hills and valleys. Three hundred twelve miles of Lake Erie shoreline stretch across two-thirds of

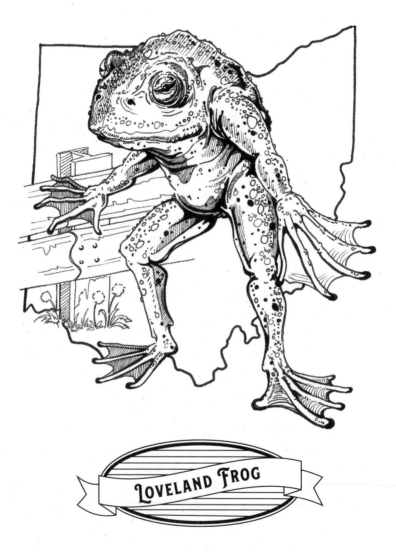

LOVELAND FROG

the northern section of the state. More than 8.1 million acres of Ohio lay under the cover of trees. That's a lot of room for, oh I don't know, Bigfoot, maybe?

Ohio Grassman

Although stories of hairy men in the forests of Ohio go back to the native Indians, the first written report, "A Gorilla in Ohio," appeared in newspapers in 1869. The creature apparently pounced upon a wagon and attacked the driver. The man's daughter, who was also in the wagon, struck the creature in the ear with a rock, and it fled.

Although scattered reports continued over the years, the sighting of a seven-foot-tall, three-hundred-pound, hairy apelike creature near Minerva in 1978 brought the Ohio Grassman to national attention, according to *Altered Dimensions* magazine. A group of children claimed to see the creature in a gravel pit. The sightings soon became regular. Evelyn Clayton, the grandmother of the children who made the initial claim, saw the creature picking through garbage in broad daylight, although she couldn't see any features through the thick mat of hair over its face.

The Clayton family continued to see the creature. On August 21 of that year, the Claytons saw what they called "panthers" in their yard, right before an enormous upright creature stepped in front of the cats. The Claytons went inside to grab firearms when one of them saw the monster leering through a kitchen window. When they went outside with the guns, the hairy creature was gone, although it left a horrendous stench.

The Claytons and neighbors continued to see the creature at night, and during the day. Authorities searching the area found two dogs with snapped necks. Bigfoot investigators discovered large footprints and grassy nests where they said the creature bedded down, giving the legendary creature the name Grassman.

Another rash of sightings of the creature occurred in the summer of 1980, although nothing has rivaled the encounters of 1978.

Mill Lake Monster

This beast was seen only once, way back in 1959, and the three teens that encountered it were happy it stayed put.

Charles Mill Lake at Charles Mill Lake Park is a man-made reservoir built in the 1930s by damming the Black Fork River. It's a popular area for fishing, boating, and hunting. On March 28, 1959, three friends, Michael Lane, Dennis Patterson, and Wayne Armstrong, were at the lake when a creature they claimed was at least seven feet tall rose straight up from the water and approached them, according to the *Columbus Navigator*. They described the beast as humanoid, but without arms. It had glowing green eyes and huge webbed feet. Terrified, they drove off, and straight to local law enforcement to report the encounter.

Police found tracks at the spot where the boys saw the being. The prints looked like they had been made with swim fins. The monster, however, was long gone. And that would be the end of the Mill Lake Monster except for a brief report by cryptozoologist Loren Coleman in his book *Curious Encounters*, where he states simply a humanoid, green-eyed monster was seen at the lake in 1963.

Orange Eyes

If there's a monster at Charles Mill Lake Reservoir, at least it's not lonely. In 1963, a number of witnesses reported seeing an eleven-foot-tall, thousand-pound apelike creature with glowing orange eyes at the park. Local legend has it the monster once lived in a tunnel beneath a nearby cemetery, but when a highway came through in the 1940s, it had to look for somewhere else to live—and it wasn't happy about it. Another sighting came in 1968 when children saw the monster in the woods, but that about did it for Orange Eyes. The beast showed itself to two fishermen in 1991 before it faded into obscurity.

The Loveland Frogs

In 1955, a man driving near the Miami River near Loveland just before 4:00 a.m. saw three humanlike figures on the side of the road. He pulled over to help them, then realized what he saw. They were creatures about four feet tall with webbed hands and feet and green, leatherlike skin. The faces of the beasts looked like frogs. The largest frogman held some kind of wand over its head, which began spitting sparks. The driver hit the accelerator, and sped away. But that wasn't the only encounter with the frogmen.

In 1972, a Loveland police officer driving on a lonely road was startled when a creature about three feet tall jumped from the side of the road, and dashed to the other side on two legs. It jumped over the guardrail, and into the Miami River. Soon after, another police officer stopped to move what he thought was a dead animal from the road when the lump leapt up and ran. The officer shot and wounded the beast, although it too escaped into the river.

Bessie

With so much shoreline on a body of water as big as Lake Erie, there's bound to be a monster in there somewhere. With a surface area of 9,940 square miles, Lake Erie is big.

The first sighting of Bessie dates back to 1793, when the captain of the ship *Felicity* saw an enormous snakelike head emerge from the surface of Lake Erie. He estimated the neck alone to be more than sixteen feet long. In 1817, people on another ship saw a forty-foot-long sea serpent, and yet another crew that same year saw one estimated to be sixty feet long.

The entire crew of a ship heading to Toledo in 1892 saw a sea serpent that appeared to be "wrestling…as if fighting with an unseen foe." They said the monster was about fifty feet long, with brown skin and large flippers.

Sightings continued into the twentieth century, with some as recently as 1993. A $100,000 reward for the capture of Bessie has been on the table for years, although Bessie remains a free serpent.

Mothman

People in Gallipolis saw a man-sized humanoid bird between November 1966 and December 1967. A newspaper reporter dubbed the creature Mothman, and it's been the subject of books, a 2002 movie starring Richard Gere, and an annual festival. I don't want to discount Ohio's part in the Mothman story, so I'm bringing it up here. However, the entity is more associated with Point Pleasant, West Virginia, so we'll revisit Mothman in exactly thirteen states.

CHAPTER 36
OKLAHOMA

THE SOONER STATE IS a midsize state nestled in the center of the US. It got the nickname "Sooner" because some early residents cheated on land claims when they settled in prime spots sooner than they were supposed to. The name Oklahoma comes from two Choctaw Indian words: *okla* (red) and *humma* (people). Although a large part of Oklahoma is covered in red dirt prairies, the state is also home to mesas and forests. Famous residents include astronaut Gordon Cooper, actor Chuck Norris, baseball great Mickey Mantle, humorist Will Rogers, and a deadly freshwater octopus.

Oklahoma Octopus

The octopus is not a freshwater creature, but since before the white man settled Oklahoma, there have been legends of deadly monsters the size of horses living in Oklahoma waters. Although the native Indians thought these monsters to be more akin to

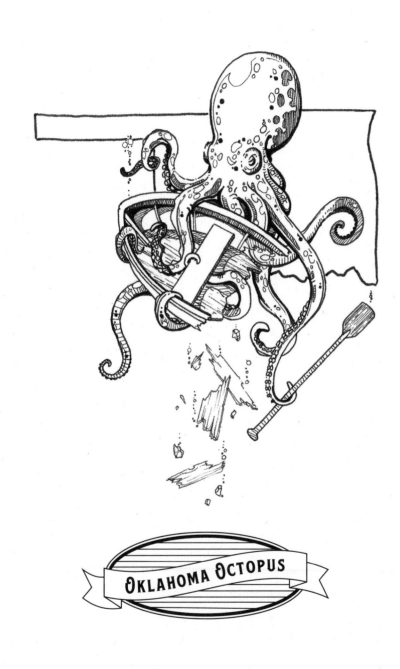

OKLAHOMA OCTOPUS

giant leeches, over the decades they've become associated with the octopus.

The octopi are said to inhabit Lake Thunderbird, Lake Oolagah, and Lake Tenkiller. People who've claimed to see the octopus say it is as big as a Jeep with reddish-brown skin—some witnesses say it looks like a shark with tentacles. The legend of the octopus has grown in Oklahoma due to an increased rate of unexplained drownings, according to *Scientific American* magazine.

The octopus reportedly "drags swimmers down with its many strong arms." Although intrigued with the idea, the magazine maintains that an octopus simply couldn't adapt to a freshwater environment. Scientists are no fun.

El Reno Chicken Man

In December 1970, near the town of El Reno just west of Oklahoma City, a farmer walked out to his chicken coop, and found the door lying on the ground, ripped off its hinges. The door and the interior of the chicken coop were covered in humanlike handprints—about seven inches long and five inches wide. The farmer called the game warden, and the warden, not knowing what to make of the scene, called the Oklahoma City Zoo.

Zoo director Lawrence Curtis said the prints (with an obviously deformed thumb) were definitely primate. "It resembles a gorilla," Curtis told the Associated Press. "It appears that whatever was making these prints was walking on all fours. There were some footprints outside."

Bare footprints—in December.

Various reports of similar prints were received throughout the state that year. The prints were shown to various wildlife experts who all agreed they were left by a primate, but what primate left them remains a mystery. However, reports of big hairy primates (Bigfoot) abound in Oklahoma to this day.

Elkman

Nick, who is a photographer, was visiting the fifty-nine-thousand-acre Wichita Mountains National Wildlife Refuge just west of Lawton in 2012 when he and a friend saw something they wished they hadn't. Around 10:00 p.m., while taking photographs of stars, they noticed the wildlife began to move. Coyotes, American bison, and a herd of elk trotted past Nick and his friend. The beasts walked past the men, some as close as five feet. Then came dangerous feral hogs, which ran by seemingly oblivious to the humans.

"It became deathly silent, and the air became ominous, and we felt an odd pressure; we started packing everything into my trunk quickly," Nick said.

The men got in the car and started to pull out, when they saw what had caused the animals to spook. "My headlights lighted up a human figure with a head I cannot easily describe."

The creature didn't look human. "It was as though it had the head of a buffalo or an elk, while standing upright with two legs and two arms that were human," he said. But the eyes were what terrified him. "The eyes were a dark red."

Terror consumed Nick, and he didn't know if he was looking at a beast or a man in a mask. As the car's headlights moved over the creature, it jerked as if hit. Nick punched the accelerator and tore away from this red-eyed monster.

Boar Man

The Wichita Mountains National Wildlife Refuge doesn't have a shortage of monsters. The preserve, designated as such in 1901 by President William McKinley, is a habitat for grazing animals like American bison, Rocky Mountain elk, and longhorn cattle. There's also more than 22,400 acres open for hiking, camping, mountain climbing and, apparently, monster encounters.

The United States government planted the refuge's Parallel Forest during the Great Depression in an attempt to combat the erosion of the Dust Bowl. The sixteen-acre forest consists of more than twenty thousand red cedar trees, each planted six feet apart, which gives the forest an eerie feel. It's said to be the home of the Boar Man.

People have seen the Boar Man for decades. The most common report is of a strong middle-aged man with pig eyes. The entity is between six and eight feet tall wearing a pig skin and carrying the tusk of a wild boar it uses to attack its victims. Some witnesses claim the Boar Man transforms into an enormous wild pig. In either guise, it is said to gore those unfortunate enough to get too close to it. In other stories, the Boar Man is an old man who uses black magic to steal his victim's youth after piercing their flesh with a boar tusk.

Lawton Wolf Man

In the early 1970s, Lawton residents witnessed a slew of werewolf sightings in the heart of winter. It started with one man who had a heart attack when he saw a bipedal wolf at his fishpond. The sightings escalated with reports of the creature stalking the town, leaping from bushes, and chasing cars.

A police officer answered the call of a witness who claimed to get a close look at the creature. It sat on a railing outside his apartment seventeen feet off the ground. The beast's face looked as if it had been burned. The creature leapt from the railing and dashed away. In line with the Lon Chaney Jr. *Wolf Man* movies of the 1940s, this creature wore the torn remains of clothing.

CHAPTER 37
OREGON

OREGON IS NESTLED IN the northwest corner of the United States between California and Washington. The state (the ninth largest) has 363 miles of Pacific coastline, the Cascade mountain range, forests, high desert, and beautiful expanses of water, from the Columbia River, to Crater Lake (with an average depth of 1,148 feet), to the 620-foot-tall Multnomah Falls. Mount Hood is the tallest mountain in Oregon, reaching 11,249 feet. Famous people from Oregon include *The Simpsons* creator Matt Groening, actor and greatest living man Bruce Campbell, director David Fincher, and inventor of the Erector Set Alfred Carlton Gilbert. Then there are the sea monsters and if Groening had drawn them they would all be yellow with overbites.

Wally

The surface of Wallowa Lake is 4,372 feet above sea level in the Wallowa Mountains. The lake, carved during the Ice Age when glaciers pushed their way across North America, may be home

COLOSSAL CLAUDE

to a giant serpent. Local Native Americans have a legend about a horned lake monster anywhere from ten to one hundred feet long.

According to an article in an 1885 edition of the *Wallowa County Chieftain*, a prospector paddling across the river saw a creature with a long neck emerge from the water about fifty yards away from his boat. The monster had an enormous flat head that rested on a ten-foot-long neck. The thing lowed like a cow and disappeared beneath the water. Although sightings of something strange in Wallowa Lake continue, they are few and far between.

Colossal Claude

A water monster with a few more sightings in Oregon is Colossal Claude. Encounters have been reported since the 1930s—encounters with a sea serpent described as anywhere from fifteen to forty feet long, frolicking in the waters of the mouth of the Columbia River, and in the adjacent ocean.

The first report was in 1934 when crewmembers of the *Columbia River* lightship claimed to have seen a forty-foot-long creature with a horselike head in the ocean near the ship's namesake river. They watched it with binoculars. According to an article in the *Salem News*, L.A. Larson, a mate on the *Columbia River*, described it as "about forty feet long. It had a neck some eight feet long, a big round body, a mean looking tail and an evil, snaky look to its head."

The creature has been spotted at least three times in the waters near Lincoln City. The best incident is when thirty people spotted a serpent with a "slender neck, a snakelike head, and a fan-shaped tail," the *Salem News* reported.

A video shot by the Shell Oil Company off the coast of Oregon in 1963 showed a fifteen-foot-long serpent, encrusted with barnacles, swimming with a spiral motion. Although people dubbed it Martin the Monster, it sure looked like Claude.

Claude has been reported in and out of the Columbia River to this day.

Bigfoot

This wouldn't be about monsters of the Pacific Northwest without Bigfoot. According to a 2015 article in the *Oregonian* newspaper, in 1972, sightings were so common around Portland that the city had a Bigfoot hotline for reports. Unfortunately, that telephone number no longer works.

Sightings of the giant hairy hominid in Oregon date back to pre-settler times, and are too numerous to detail. There are 1,442 encounter reports on the Oregon Bigfoot website alone. However, here is the story of the one Bigfoot—the Chetco Monster.

For years prior to 1904, prospectors near Myrtle Point had reported encountering a Wildman in the woods, a Wildman that terrified them. The first encounter involved two men who heard something large walking outside their cabin. When they looked, they saw a humanlike figure, but it was too big to be a man. They dashed back inside. The Wildman grabbed onto the cabin, and shook the building while screaming, keeping the men huddled in fear until it stopped. One of the men braved opening the door to find a huge, hairy, manlike monster walking away, and took a shot at it with his rifle. In his terror, he missed.

Days later at a nearby cabin, the events repeated themselves, except the inhabitants were ready for it. They all took their guns and ran outside, only to be bombarded by rocks they estimated as being about four pounds each. The monster disappeared into the forest.

People continued to see the Chetco Monster for years: a seven-foot-tall hairy man with large feet and hands.

Dogman

Although not as plentiful as Bigfoot encounters, there have been a growing number of Dogman sightings in Oregon.

People have reported seeing a Dogman across the country, especially in Minnesota, Michigan, and Wisconsin. The reports vary from place to place. In those states, as well as Arizona and Kansas, the Dogman appears to be a large, wolflike dog that walks on two legs, and is often seen eating roadkill. In Missouri, the beast typically walks on four legs, but when seen by humans it raises to two, and slowly—confidently—walks away. In Illinois, the Dogman has been reported to look like a large dog with human hands. However, sightings in Oregon report a seven-foot-tall hairy canine biped with a humanlike face, that doesn't leave footprints. The lack of footprints associated with these Oregon Dogmen is fascinating to say the least.

Cadborosaurus

There are also reports of this mythical sea beast in Oregon, but there are more from Washington. We'll just tuck Caddy away for later.

CHAPTER 38
PENNSYLVANIA

PENNSYLVANIA, ONE OF AMERICA'S thirteen original British colonies, is a treasure trove of important points in United States history. Independence Hall in Philadelphia is the building in which the Declaration of Independence and the US Constitution were signed. Philadelphia is also home to the Liberty Bell, a symbol of American independence. Author, inventor, statesman, and founding father Benjamin Franklin died and is buried there. More modern famous residents include artist Andy Warhol, actors Will Smith and Bradley Cooper, NBA legend Kobe Bryant, and singer Taylor Swift. Pennsylvania isn't a small state, nor is it large, ranking thirty-third in size. Its geography is diverse, containing everything from mountains to inland shores, and, of course forestland. Lots and lots of forestland.

SQUONK

The Squonk

In the old-growth forests in northern Pennsylvania lurks an odd beast named Squonk. With saggy skin covered in warts, this pig-like creature hides in the woods. A pathetic being, the Squonk spends its life crying. According to legend, anyone who tries to capture the Squonk ends up standing in front of a pool of tears.

The only story of a captured Squonk is from the book *Fearsome Creatures of the Lumberwoods*, by William T. Cox. Apparently a man named J.P. Wentling snagged a Squonk in a sack, but as Wentling walked toward home, the heavy sack slowly became lighter. When Wentling looked inside, all he found was a wet spot.

Werewolves

Encounters with a seven-foot-tall, bipedal wolflike creature in Pennsylvania date back to the late 1800s when a northern Pennsylvania hunter shot a wolf. When he approached the animal, he found the body of a man dead from a bullet. Encounters with werewolves in Pennsylvania range from wolf men, to upright dogs, to wolves with human faces, and humans with wolf faces.

The following encounter in Mercer County was sent to the Dogman Field Research Organization:

In 1990, a group of friends was walking in the forest near their homes when they heard a crunching sound in the dark. One member of the group trained a flashlight on the area of the sound, and the light showed an enormous dog eating something on the ground. When the large canine became aware of the light, the creature, described as a man with a dog face, stood on its hind legs, glared at the group of friends and dashed into the trees. Some of them went back the next day and discovered a partially eaten deer carcass there.

Raystown Ray

You wouldn't think a man-made lake would be the basis of a monster story, but that's just what they have in Huntingdon County.

Raystown Lake is a twenty-eight-mile-long reservoir with a surface area of 8,300 acres, and a maximum depth near two hundred feet. It's also allegedly home to Ray. Ray was first reported in 1962 in the first incarnation of the lake. The lake had originally formed in 1905 when a dam was created to control flooding. The Army Corps of Engineers replaced that dam in 1971. The 1962 sighting nearly canceled the Raystown Ski Club Water Show. People reported seeing a fifty-foot-long "Loch Ness Monster" type creature around the ski area. It had a lizard-like head attached to a thick, serpentine neck.

Sightings are slim, but a photograph of a plesiosaur-like creature taken by a tourist in 2007 has kept the legend of Raystown Ray alive.

Tommyknockers

When the Cornish people immigrated to the United States in the 1800s, they brought with them not only a knowledge of mining, but also the knowledge of creatures that lurk in the mines—something mischievous. The Tommyknockers. Tommyknockers are two-foot-tall, green, gnome-like creatures dressed in mining gear. They live in mines and prey on miners. Sometimes the Tommyknockers are simply troublesome and steal the miners' food and tools when they're not looking. Other times these creatures are deadly.

Although the legends of these dwarfish creatures are old, the stories began in the United States in the 1820s when the Cornish miners worked in the coal mines in Pennsylvania. The legend spread during the 1849 California Gold Rush when miners moved westward.

The term Tommyknockers comes from the knocking sound miners hear prior to a cave-in. The miners attributed the sounds of shifting earth and cracking support timbers to the hammering of these dwarves. Belief in these creatures varied. Some thought if a cave-in occurred and no one was injured, the Tommyknockers were being kind. If someone died in an accident, the Tommyknockers were taking vengeance on some ill the miners caused. Still others thought following the sound of the knocking would lead them to a vein.

What the Tommyknockers were has changed over the centuries. Cornish miners originally believed the knockers were souls of those who crucified Jesus Christ. Those responsible for the crucifixion were sent to tin mines in England to work until they died. Later explanations simply involved the spirits of any worker who died in the mine.

Much like the Scandinavian tradition of leaving food for gnomes to keep the creatures from performing mischief, miners took to leaving food and tools for the Tommyknockers to thank them for warnings of danger, and to keep the warnings coming.

Albatwitch

Werewolves aren't the only hairy bipedal critters encountered in Pennsylvania. The woods around the city of Columbia are supposedly inhabited by a four-foot-tall humanlike monster called the Albatwitch.

The name is a somewhat shortened form of "apple snitch," which these creatures are known to do. The Albatwitch have a habit of stealing apples from picnic baskets, or while sitting in trees, and throwing the fruit at people—a healthier habit than their bigger, hairier cousins the Bigfoot, who are known to throw large stones.

Although most reports of encounters with these small, furry, forest dwellers are from the early history of the state, there are more recent reports from the 1950s through the 1970s of people seeing and hearing the Albatwitch.

The Butler Gargoyle

In and around Butler County, a number of people have seen what they described as a gargoyle. One encounter, reported to researcher Stan Gordon in March 2011, involved a man driving in rural Pennsylvania. He saw what he thought was a deer on the side of the road, but when he eased closer, a leather-skinned eight-foot-tall humanoid shape stood from a squat and crossed the road in three steps.

The witness described the head of the monster as sloped in the back like it wore a bicycle helmet. Its muscular arms ended in claws, and its legs bent like a bird's. But the strangest part of the creature were the wings on its back that lay flat on its body, the tips reaching up to its ears.

This wasn't the only encounter with the gargoyle. In that same month, at least six other motorists saw the Butler Gargoyle along that stretch of road.

CHAPTER 39
RHODE ISLAND

RHODE ISLAND IS THE smallest of the United States. In size, it's fiftieth out of fifty at 1,545 square miles (the same size as a single county, Marathon, in Wisconsin). It's forty-third in population density at a little more than a million. One of the original British colonies, it is called an island because the colony began on Aquidneck Island in Narragansett Bay, and Rhode because the colony was once referred to as "Isle of Rhodes." The state is home to the Ivy League Brown University, and the fictional city of Quahog in the adult television cartoon *Family Guy*. It is also the home state of *Family Guy* creator Seth MacFarlane, actors John Huston and James Franco, Olympic medalist Michelle Kwan, horror author H.P. Lovecraft, and just maybe, Bigfoot.

Bigfoot

With only 393,000 acres of forestland in Rhode Island, it isn't the perfect location for the big hairy fellow, but stories of Big

BLOCK NESS MONSTER

Rhodey have been enough to send cryptozoologists into the woods of this tiny state.

According to an article in the *Coventry Patch* newspaper, people have seen the beast near the towns of Cumberland, West Greenwich, and Exeter. Although investigators have come up with plaster casts of large footprints, patches of hair, and twisted trees, they are most encouraged by a 2011 sighting by Dina Palazini and Kris Stepney, who claim to have caught Big Rhodey on video.

The short clip shows the view taken from the cab of a moving vehicle. The trees and an ancient stone wall slowly move by when something seems to step from behind a tree.

The Block Ness Monster

In 1996, fishermen aboard the *Mad Monk* pulled their net from the water off the shores of Block Island, fourteen miles from the coast of Rhode Island, according to a story by the Associated Press. Along with the net came the fourteen-foot skeleton of what looked like a serpent. When they arrived at the dock, the fisherman sat the bones out for display at the Point Judith ferry.

New York state park biologist Lee Scott came to the island to inspect the skeleton. According to the article, Scott remembered saying, "What the heck is this?" when he looked at the find.

Although at the time shark specialists were certain the remains were of a basking shark, no one can be certain what type of creature the Block Ness Monster really was. Shortly after it was found, "kidnappers" stole it to preserve the monster's short legacy, which consisted of tourists, T-shirts, and "Block Ness cocktails."

Sea Monster of Teddy's Beach

In 2007, a group of people visited Teddy's Beach in Portsmouth to fish and swim. The peaceful day changed when the swimmers encountered something enormous in the water.

According to WPRI 12 Eyewitness News, Rachel Carney was floating in the water beyond the swimming area of the beach when a fifteen-foot-long creature began to swim around her. As the thing began circling, Carney felt it was toying with her, but at least she got a good look at it. It had greenish-black skin with a white underside and teeth at least four inches long. It kept ducking its head under the water. Each time it rose above the surface, it hissed at her.

"I was deep out in the water and kept hearing this hissing sound," she told WPRI. "Then I saw its head come up showing me its big teeth. It kept rolling while it was swimming and knocking into my feet. I just froze."

Her fiancé, Dennis Vasconcellos, swam out to Carney, and pulled her away from the sea serpent. "This thing was big," he told the news station. "I mean its head was almost the size of a basketball."

By the time Vasconcellos pulled Carney to safety, others on the beach were rushing loved ones from the water.

Scientists were baffled at the description of the sea monster.

Vampire

In 1892, the family of George and Mary Brown of Exeter became stricken with tuberculosis, known then as consumption. Superstition overruled science in many people during the Victorian era, so townspeople thought the consumption curse on the family was due to evil undead.

Two family members who had succumbed to consumption were exhumed and looked decomposed, as they should. However, George and Mary's daughter Mercy, who had been entombed in an aboveground vault, had not decomposed at all. People grabbed this as evidence that Mercy was a vampire who rose from the crypt to suck the life out of her family members as they slept.

The people removed Mercy's heart and burned it. They mixed the ashes with water and fed them to her brother Edwin, believing this would stop the undead from feasting on him in the night. Edwin died from tuberculosis anyway.

CHAPTER 40
SOUTH CAROLINA

SOUTH CAROLINA, ONE OF the original thirteen British colonies, was the first to ratify the original US Constitution (the Articles of Confederation) in 1781, and was the first state to vote to leave the United States during the Civil War in 1860 (don't worry, it came back). South Carolina is known for many other firsts for the US. The first round of golf in the New World was played in Charleston; the first symphony orchestra was organized in the state, as were the first public college and the first museum. Famous people born in South Carolina include US president Andrew Jackson, the Godfather of Soul James Brown, comedian Chris Rock, and baseball great Shoeless Joe Jackson. It's not a big state (fortieth largest), or the most populous (ranked twenty-third), but the geography consists of sandy beaches, marshes, the Piedmont Plateau, rivers, and lakes, so what it lacks in size it makes up for in beauty. The state has more than 683 square miles of lake surface, which makes it a perfect home for a lizard man.

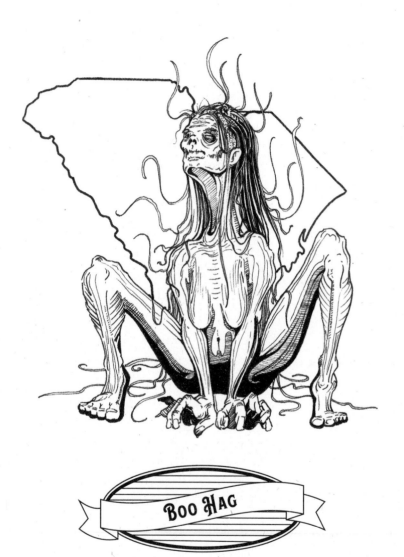

BOO HAG

Lizard Man

On June 29, 1988, at around 2:00 a.m., a tire blew out on seventeen-year-old Christopher Davis's car. He pulled to the side of the road that ran along Scrape Ore Swamp to change the tire. As he finished the work, a thumping approached him from behind. When Davis turned toward the noise, he found a seven-foot-tall creature running at him. He leapt into the car and started to drive away, but not before he got a good look at it. The thick creature ran on two legs like a man. Black hair covered the monster along with patches of lizard skin on its three-toed hands and feet. The lizard man reached for the car, but missed as Davis swerved out of the way. It then launched itself onto the roof. Davis continued to swerve, trying to throw it off. When he arrived home, he found the rearview mirror damaged and scratch marks crisscrossing the roof of the car, according to the *Charleston Post and Courier*.

When Davis's father took Chris to the Lee County Sheriff's Office more than two weeks later to file a report, they discovered this wasn't the only such case in the area.

On July 14, sheriff's deputies responded to the home of Tom and Mary Wave in a small community outside Bishopville on a call of vehicular vandalism. Chrome was torn from the body of the car, as were the antenna and hood ornament. Wires under the hood of the vehicle had been chewed on. Stranger yet, the car was covered with muddy footprints. It was then that locals told the officers of many recent sightings of a seven-foot-tall monster with red eyes in the Bishopville area.

Lizard man encounters soon began to spring up all over the area, and officials attempted to track the creature, but all they found were large, three-toed footprints. Although rare, lizard man sightings continue to this day.

Third Eye Man

Two students wandering the University of South Carolina utility tunnels (dubbed "the Catacombs") on November 12, 1949, witnessed something strange—a man wearing silver clothing. The man didn't look at the students as he lifted up a manhole cover, and climbed into the hole. One of the students, Christopher Nichols, was a student reporter and wrote the story for the campus newspaper the *Gamecock*. In April that next year a campus officer making late night rounds found mutilated chickens, and a man in silver clothing hunched over them.

But the officer armed with a flashlight got a better look at the silver-clad figure than did the students. The man's skin was "gray and grotesque," and he had a third eye in the center of his forehead. The officer called for backup, but when the second policeman arrived, the Third Eye Man had escaped into the tunnel system.

The Third Eye Man became the stuff of legend around the Gamecock campus for almost two decades before it became reality again. Fraternity brothers hazing pledges in the 1960s by taking them into the Catacombs for a fright saw what looked like a crippled old man dressed in silver. When they approached him, the man struck them with a pipe, knocking one student to the floor of the tunnel before escaping.

A spokesman for the University of South Carolina told a reporter for the student newspaper that there's nothing in the service tunnels that shouldn't be there but empty beer bottles.

Boo Hag

After slavery was abolished in the United States, some of the former African slaves settled on America's East Coast from North Carolina to Florida. The mixing of traditions and legends brought from various regions of Africa created a unique culture, the Gullah. One legend of the Gullah from the coast of South Carolina and islands close to the coast is the Boo Hag. The Boo Hag is a vampire that doesn't feed on blood, but instead sits on the chest of its sleeping victim and sucks a person's strength through their breath.

Boo Hags can enter the victim's home through any sort of small opening, and when they do, this creature—which appears as an old woman with no skin—sits on the victim's chest and "rides" them. The Boo Hag victim will then wake exhausted. Although these red demons usually leave their victims alive so they can feed on them again, when they take all the strength they can, the Boo Hags steal the victim's skin and wear it as clothing.

If you think a Boo Hag may be riding you at night, there is a defense. Sleep with a broom next to your bed. The Boo Hag will spend so much time counting the individual pieces of straw it won't attack you.

A popular good night saying among the Gullah is, "Don't let de hag ride ya."

Messie, the Lake Murray Monster

At the time of its construction (1927 to 1930), Lake Murray was the largest man-made reservoir in the world. At forty-one miles long and fourteen miles wide, it's still pretty big, with a surface area of fifty thousand acres, and a maximum depth of about two hundred feet. It's the right size to hide a monster, but as a man-made lake, the creature dubbed "Messie" understandably has its doubters.

The first sighting of Messie was in 1933 when Gilbert Little of Ballentine claimed to see something large swimming in the lake. The most famous encounter, according to the book *Weird Carolinas* by Roger Manly, was when something attacked the boat of Buddy and Shirley Browning. The couple had been fishing with their friend Kord Brazell when something the size of an alligator ("It was not an alligator," Buddy protested) aggressively approached the trio.

"It tried to climb into the boat," Shirley said in the book's account. "Buddy beat it off with a paddle."

Although Buddy didn't know what the creature was (he thought it might be a sturgeon), he docked, and went back to his house for a shotgun. "We was going to go back after it and claim it, but we never did see it again."

In 1980, the newspaper the *Independent News* described Messie as a combination of a "snake and something prehistoric."

In 1990, retired army general Marvin B. Corder told the South Carolina Department of Natural Resources that he and his son had encountered a "serpentlike creature" about "forty to sixty feet long" with the "tail of an eel."

The Pink Mess of Goose Creek Lagoon

A December 7, 1948, article in the *St. Petersburg (Florida) Times* recounted a twenty-year-old story by novelist and naturalist Herbert Ravenel Sass, who witnessed a pink "amphibious mess" in floodwaters near the Goose Creek Lagoon.

According to Sass's account, he and his wife were in a flat-bottomed boat when they saw, "moving through the water growths below the surface an indeterminate shape." When the boat was almost over the shape, Sass slipped a paddle under it and lifted it above the water. "It was very heavy, about the thickness of a man's lower thigh, of a bright salmon pink and orange color. How long it was I don't know, because both ends remained under water." Although Sass and his wife didn't see a head or tail, they both saw a pair of legs, "like an alligator's or salamander's."

"It may be … fantastic to suggest," the newspaper quoted Sass as saying, "that there exists in these Carolina swamps and lagoons a species of giant amphibian of which no specimen has yet been taken."

Bigfoot

With thirteen million acres of forestland, South Carolina is a prime spot for Bigfoot sightings. Although encounters with this big hairy fellow stretch back to pre-colonial times, with the encroachment of civilization came fewer encounters. According to a 2014 article in the *Free Times* of Columbia, South Carolina, the Bigfoot Field Researchers Organization lists only "fifty Bigfoot reports in South Carolina dating back to 1968."

But physical sightings, footprints, wood knocking, and gorilla-type nests have all been reported from the forested areas of the state. A group of cryptozoology enthusiasts in South Carolina, the Carolina Cryptid Crew, recorded what they claim to be Bigfoot cries around 3:00 a.m. in March 2015 in Oconee County.

CHAPTER 41
SOUTH DAKOTA

SOUTH DAKOTA IS A state in the midwestern US. It's the seventeenth largest of the United States, but the fifth least populated. Famous residents include TV game show host Bob Barker, Vice President Hubert Humphrey, TV journalist Tom Brokaw, and Charlie's Angel Cheryl Ladd. It's also home to Wall Drug Store. Located on the edge of the Badlands in the town of Wall, people as far away as France, Afghanistan, Australia, and Antarctica (mostly a few hundred bored climate scientists) know how many miles they are from this tourist destination. The store that originally attracted travelers with free water as far back as the 1930s has more than three thousand signs around the world. If you haven't seen one, you haven't looked very hard. The state's rolling plains to the east are covered in fields and ranches, eventually giving way to the stark beauty of the Badlands and the Black Hills. The Black Hills aren't hills; they comprise a low mountain range that features the carvings of four US presidents (Washington, Jefferson, Lincoln, and Teddy Roosevelt), and the

BANSHEE OF THE BADLANDS

partially completed Crazy Horse Memorial. A large pocket of mammoth remains was discovered near the city of Hot Springs in 1974. Although there are no more mammoths tromping through South Dakota (maybe), there could be dinosaurs.

Living Dinosaurs

Living fossils may still roam South Dakota. In 1934, a large dinosaur-like creature lumbered onto a road near Lake Campbell in eastern South Dakota, forcing a farmer to swerve his tractor to miss it, which caused the farmer to drive the tractor into a ditch. When the farmer came back with help, people discovered a trail of unidentifiable tracks from a large, four-legged beast that went through a muddy field, and continued toward the lake. Before this sighting, livestock had been mysteriously disappearing from the area. Unfortunately, there was no follow-up to this story.

However, if you want to see a dinosaur in South Dakota, swing on over to Wall Drug for a mechanical *Tyrannosaurus rex* that pushes its head from a patch of palms, then roars.

Taku-He

The Taku-He is South Dakota's Bigfoot. Although this beast fits the typical physical description of a Bigfoot as a smelly hair-covered giant, the Taku-He has a worse attitude than most Bigfoot, and may also be a snappy dresser. Some people have reported seeing the tall, hairy, apelike creature wearing a coat and tall hat.

Although there were Taku-He reports from early in the 1970s (specifically on September 6, 1974, near Jefferson, when a man saw a Bigfoot dragging a dead animal through an alfalfa field), sightings of the South Dakota Bigfoot increased dramatically in 1977.

In September of that year, ranch hands near Little Eagle saw a big gorilla watching them run cattle. When the men approached the creature, it ran away. The encounters didn't stop there. More than twenty-five reports came from the area around Little Eagle over the next three months. Some of the encounters put the Taku-He in the vicinity of mutilated livestock whose genitals had been removed, and the animals drained of blood.

The Little Devils of Spirit Mound

In the southeast corner of South Dakota is a 1,280-foot-tall, 320-acre hill that is the highest point on the Great Plains in a one-hundred-mile radius. The Sioux, Omaha, and Otoes Indians revered and feared the Spirit Mound, believing "Little Devils" dwelled within. The devils, eighteen-inch-tall people, hated humankind. One legend has hundreds of Indian warriors attacking the Little Devils' home on the mound. The diminutive creatures slaughtered the war party with magical arrows.

During their historic westward expedition, explorers Meriwether Lewis and William Clark visited the mound to look for the Little Devils. Lewis, Clark, and ten others from the expedition traveled three hours from their camp by the Missouri River to Spirit Mound.

"This Mound is Situated on an elevated plain in a leavel and extensive prarie," Clark wrote in his journal (grammatical and spelling errors are Clark's). "The base of the Mound is a regular parallelogram ... The reagular form of this hill would in Some measure justify a belief that it owed its Orrigin to the hand of man; but as the earth and loos pebbles and other Substances of which it was Composed, bare an exact resemblance to the Steep

Ground which border on the Creek in its neighborhood we Concluded it was most probably the production of nature—."

Sergeant John Ordway's journal revealed that although the party "found none of the little people," they discovered "several holes in the ground" which were large enough for the Little Devils to hide in.

Today the Spirit Mound is a state park covered in native prairie grass.

Banshee of the Badlands

The Badlands of South Dakota open from seemingly nowhere. The rolling plains of the rest of the state suddenly give way to a dramatic series of spires and canyons dotted by bighorn sheep, bison, and prairie dogs. Fossils are commonly found in this ancient seabed, the strata as easily visible as the layers of a cake.

Something lonely roams this desolate area in the southwest part of the state, specifically around a butte known as Watch Dog. Called the Banshee of the Badlands, the shriek of this entity pierces the soul of anyone who hears it. The creature looks like a woman, but anyone who sees it knows it is no woman. The scream pierces the night and has terrified travelers, cowboys, and immigrants for the past century and a half.

A banshee is a creature of Irish folklore whose scream predicates the death of someone in the family. Why one would be in the middle of America is anyone's guess.

Lake Kampeska Monster

In 1888, a group having a picnic at Lake Kampeska in eastern South Dakota was surprised when a monster broke the surface of the water, and ruined a perfectly good lunch. The lizard–like creature was at least two hundred feet long, according to the witnesses. The beast had a thirty-foot-long fluked tail and a "crested head as large as a yearling calf," they reported to the *Watertown Public Opinion* newspaper. The monster was covered in scales.

"Opening its awful jaws (it) uttered the most unearthly laugh that ever broke on mortal ears," one witness told the *Public Opinion*. The picnickers, all well educated and sure of what they saw, left everything on the lakeshore and hurried home.

Although this was the biggest sighting of the monster in this 5,250-acre inland glacial lake, people aboard an excursion boat saw something similar on the lake two years before, according to *South Dakota* magazine.

Two-Faced Monster

Native American mothers spoke of the Two-Faced Monster in sharp tones to keep their children close when the sun went down. The monster would nab over-confident children, or in some cases pregnant women, and stab them to death with its knife-like elbows.

The Plains, Sioux, Lakota, and Omaha Indians all have legends of the Two-Faced Monster. Lakota legends claim Two-Face was once a beautiful woman who tried to seduce the god of the sun, and was given two faces as punishment—one beautiful, one disfigured and ugly. Anyone who sees both faces of this monster dies instantly. Or so the stories go.

CHAPTER 42
TENNESSEE

THE SOUTHEASTERN STATE OF Tennessee is the birthplace of bluegrass music, Mountain Dew soda, miniature golf, the tow truck, and Jack Daniels Whiskey. It's tied with Missouri as the state that borders the most other states (eight). It's also the thirty-sixth-largest state, but the seventeenth most populous. Famous Tennesseans include singers Johnny Cash, Aretha Franklin and Tina Turner; actor Morgan Freeman; director Quentin Tarantino; former vice president Al Gore; and pro wrestling legend Ric Flair (Woooooo). Oak Ridge, Tennessee, was established in the 1940s as part of the Manhattan Project that produced the first atomic bomb. This 440-mile-long state features plains, lakes, rivers, and mountains, and is the perfect place for the Tennessee Wildman.

WHITE SCREAMER

Tennessee Wildman

In the late 1800s, residents of McNairy County encountered a creature that wasn't quite a man, but was not quite a Bigfoot either. The beast was reportedly seven feet tall with either dark gray or dark red hair, fiery red eyes, and its hair and beard hung to its waist. The creature's scream, witnesses said, could freeze a man's blood. Amazingly strong and fast, the Wildman often targeted women with its threats, although none of its attacks were successful, according to the May 5, 1871, edition of the *Hagerstown Mail*. The Wildman was also known to silently approach houses, but if it was seen it took off running, effortlessly leaping fences before it disappeared into nearby trees.

Although Wildman reports have continued over the decades, the last recorded sighting was in the 1990s in Carter County, on the opposite side of the state from McNairy County.

Paranormal investigator Robb Phillips appeared on the television program *Monsters and Mysteries in America* and described his encounter with the Tennessee Wildman at the Watauga Cliffs.

Walking toward the cliffs in the rain, Phillips and his cousin froze when the tenor of the forest changed. "It was like everything in the woods just stopped," Phillips told the local newspaper, the *Elizabethton*. "There was no sound at all. Then we heard twigs snapping, and then there was this scream. It was like nothing we had ever heard before. It was not a human sound or an animal sound. Then we took off." As they fled through the woods, the cousins saw the source of the scream—a smelly manlike hairy beast at least nine feet tall with red eyes.

"We knew we had experienced something," Phillips told the *Elizabethton*. "We had heard the rumors, but when it actually happened, we knew it wasn't a myth."

The Flintville Monster

A creature that more fits the description of a Bigfoot has been sighted for years in the Tennessee foothills. According to the *Augusta Chronicle*, this seven-foot-tall monster smells like a skunk and leaves footprints sixteen inches long. One victim told the newspaper the hairy monster screamed like an ape as it chased him through the forest. Unlike Bigfoot, who is often depicted as a gentle giant, this beast seen around the town of Flintville is aggressive. "That thing's so big it could easily hurt somebody," farmer Ned Sinclair told the *Chronicle*.

The first encounter with the Flintville Monster occurred in 1976 when an enormous manlike ape jumped on the hood of a woman's car, breaking the radio antenna. It hooted and jumped on the roof before it leapt off and dashed into the woods. Attacks continued into the 1980s when the beast chased a woman into her house and banged on her door. But a number of attacks involved cars, including the account of a plumber and the pastor of a local church, who each reported different encounters with a Bigfoot-like beast that broke their vehicle antennas, and bashed in the windshields.

The most notable account occurred in 1976 when the mother of a four-year-old saw the tall, hairy creature running across a field toward her son who played in the yard. She bolted from the house to intercept it. "It reached out its long, hairy arms toward Gary and came within a few inches of him," she told investigators at the time. She reached her son before the creature, grabbed him, and bolted back inside the house, where she called police. A hunting party searched for the Flintville Monster but found only enormous footprints, and blood.

White Screamer

A misty creature lurks near the small town of White Bluff, Tennessee—a creature of legend. As the story goes, in the 1920s, a man built a farm home for his family of nine in a hollow near the town. Every night after the family went to sleep, a wailing shriek would pierce the night, rousing the household. Finally, the man had enough of the night screaming and bolted outside with his shotgun to track down the thing that tormented his family. As he followed the scream, it led him back to his house, where the screams changed into the death wails of his family. When he rushed into the home, he found his wife and seven children torn to bits.

The White Screamer is similar to the banshee of Irish folklore, which foretells death, and has been known to follow families. Since the Irish are the third-largest ethnic group in Tennessee, maybe some banshees made it to the United States from across the pond.

The Tennessee Terror

The 651.8-mile-long Tennessee River is supposed to be home to a twenty-five-foot-long river beast. The legend began in 1822; a farmer was fishing in the river when a "sea serpent" emerged from surface of the water and scared him so badly he died soon after. Another fisherman told a similar story in 1827 when he encountered the Tennessee Terror and it almost shook him out of his canoe. The man described the creature as bluish-yellow and built like a giant snake.

The legend has grown over the years, turning the Tennessee Terror into a giant catfish called Catzilla that has grown to at least five hundred pounds. Although species of catfish in Spain and Southeast Asia grow to that size, science knows of no species that big to swim the waters of Tennessee—at least not yet.

Hairy Human on Four Legs

Tennessee is home to many reports of a four-foot-long entity with a human face that walks on four legs. A woman exploring an undisclosed cave reported seeing the creature climbing along a cave wall. The monster had brown eyes and was covered with brown hair. Its short legs ended in "paws."

A report of a similar creature was made by a group of people walking on a wooded trail in Marion County. The hairy monster on four legs walked toward them on the trail and stopped to look at them—it had a human face.

CHAPTER 43
TEXAS

TEXAS IS THE SECOND-LARGEST state in the US. It's so big, Texas's one-time tourism slogan was "Texas—It's Like A Whole Other Country." At 268,580 square miles, the state is slightly bigger than France. It boasts four city areas (Dallas-Fort Worth counts as one) that rank in the top ten most populous cities in America. There are still cowboys in Texas, as well as oilmen, and for some reason hipsters. Texas calls itself the Lone Star State to celebrate the fact that it was once an independent republic, even though it's also been under the flags of Spain, France, Mexico, the American Confederacy, and the United States. Famous people from Texas include actress Carol Burnett; US president Lyndon B. Johnson; jockey Willie Shoemaker; Major League Baseball Hall of Fame pitcher Nolan Ryan; aviation mogul Howard Hughes; singers Roy Orbison, Willie Nelson, and Buddy Holly; *Conan the Barbarian* author Robert E. Howard; and *Star Trek* creator Gene Roddenberry. The landscape of

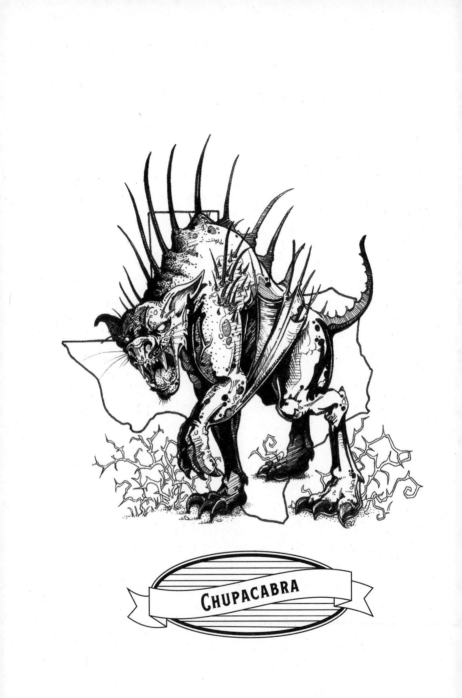

CHUPACABRA

Texas is as vast as its size. There are deserts, swamps, grasslands, piney woods, hills, prairies, forests, beaches, mountains, and plenty of room for monsters to go a-roamin'.

The Lake Worth Monster

The area around Lake Worth, a 3,489-acre reservoir in Fort Worth, is home to a half-man/half-goat creature called the Lake Worth Monster. Variations of an urban legend set in the 1930s tell of either Klansmen or drunken rednecks crossing a bridge that connects the cities of Lewisville and Alton, and lynching a black farmer known by the locals as the Goatman. Although they hanged the man over the bridge, when they pulled up the rope, the man was no longer attached. Although the bridge is no longer open to vehicle traffic, legends persist that crossing the bridge at night will bring the wrath of the Goatman.

Then, decades later, people started to see a goat-like biped in the area, and the legend of the Goatman came to life.

In July 1969, couples making out in their cars parked near the bridge encountered a creature that walked like a man, but looked like a satyr from Greek mythology. After they reported this sighting to the police, another local man claimed a half-man/half-goat jumped onto his car from a tree, leaving an eighteen-inch scratch in the paint. Although police couldn't say the Goatman caused the scratch, the damage was indeed there.

The last sighting from that year involved ten people gathered near the lake one October night when the Goatman appeared atop a bluff and threw an old tire at them. A man named Allen Plaster took a Polaroid photograph of the event, according to NBC 5 in Dallas-Fort Worth.

Although 1969 was an active time for Goatman sightings, encounters have slowed to a trickle, and the Lake Worth Monster has receded back into the shadows of legend.

La Lechuza

Tales of tragedies changing humans into something other than human abound in Texas, like the story of La Lechuza from El Paso. *La Lechuza* means "the owl" in Spanish, but in local stories it means the Owl Witch.

As legend has it, after locals discovered a woman practicing dark magic, they put her to death. However, her magic was strong, and the woman came back to life. During the day she appears as a woman dressed in black, but at night she assumes the form of a human-sized owl with the woman's face.

The Owl Witch spends the night searching for prey, sometimes luring unsuspecting people into the dark by whistling or wailing like a baby. When the person goes to investigate the sound, she snatches them and carries them to their death.

Although fanciful, stories abound of people seeing giant black birds at night that follow them home; the next morning, the people wake to find scratches around their windows. In one story, people suspected their neighbor, an old woman, of being a witch. One night when an enormous black bird threatened neighborhood children, a man took out his rifle and shot it. Although the neighbors kept close watch on the old woman's house, she didn't appear for days. When she finally did, she walked with a pronounced limp.

Black-Eyed Kids

The term "Black-Eyed Kids" hit popular culture on January 16, 1998, when journalist Brian Bethel posted his encounter with children whose eyes were black, with no iris or white.

Bethel was sitting in his car across from a movie theater in Abilene at 9:45 p.m. when he heard a tap on his window. Two boys between the ages of ten and fourteen stood outside, staring at him. "An overwhelming sense of fear and unearthliness rushed in," Bethel wrote in his post.

The boys insisted Bethel drive them home. "Let us in," one said. "We can't get in your car until you do, you know. Just let us in." As Bethel began to open the door, he saw the boys' pure black eyes. "Just two staring orbs," he wrote. Bethel jerked away from the door and drove quickly out of the parking lot. When he looked behind him, the sidewalk was empty—the boys were gone.

More than a decade and a half later, Bethel still doesn't know what he encountered. "I honestly wish I could explain this away," Bethel said. "I've tried to come up with any number of scenarios, from my eyes being temporarily dilated from the brightness of the theater marquee to me just plain not seeing things properly. Most of the time, I try to just push this particular event back into my subconscious, but it is always there."

Big Bird

In the early months of the year 1976, people from along the Rio Grande Valley up to nearby San Antonio claim to have seen a bird as large as a man flying through the Texas sky. The first reports were from policemen in Harlingen who saw a bird flying over the road with a wingspan wider than their patrol cars. This story was quickly followed by a more terrifying one. According to the *San Antonio Current*, two teenagers, Jackie Davies and Tracy Lawson, were playing in the Lawsons' backyard when they noticed a five-foot-tall bird with the face of a gorilla standing in a nearby irrigation canal staring at them. Lawson's parents later found huge three-toed bird tracks on the banks of the canal.

Stories from that year continued. Something large slammed into the wall of Brownsville resident Alverco Guajardo's trailer. When he ran outside with a knife, he found himself face-to-face with a man-sized bird. Another Brownsville resident saw Big Bird, but claimed it had a bald head and red glowing eyes. He told the *Brownsville Herald* at the time, "I was scared. It's got wings like a bird, but it's not a bird. That animal is not of this world." San Benito policeman Arturo Padilla saw a five-foot-tall bird with a twelve-foot wingspan that matched that description in the headlights of his police car.

The sightings continued when a man in Raymondville heard a strange noise outside his home and walked outside to investigate, only to be attacked by an enormous bird with a bald head. The creature grabbed his shoulders and tried to lift him off the ground, but the man squirmed free and fell to the ground. Neighbors came to investigate the screams and found him on the ground trembling, his shirt ripped.

The sightings stopped soon after.

Pterodactyl

More than just bald, gorilla-faced giant birds flew in the Texas skies in 1976. That February, three San Antonio elementary school teachers were terrorized by a creature with a wingspan of between fifteen and twenty feet that swooped over their car. The creature seemed to glide rather than fly on enormous bat-like wings. The teachers all described the creature as a pterodactyl, and teachers should know what a pterodactyl looks like, even though they also should know these flying dinosaurs died out more than sixty-five million years ago.

The teachers weren't alone. In September 1982, on State Highway 100 near Los Fresnos, James Thompson stopped his vehicle and watched what looked like a black featherless bird flying low, according to the book *The Truth About Dinosaurs: The Witness of Creation Series Volume Five*, by Billy Crone. The creature, with a wingspan of about six feet, had a hump on its head, and its skin was leathery. When Thompson researched the creature he'd seen, he was stunned to see it had been a pterodactyl.

Mountain Boomer

On the subject of living dinosaurs, from Big Bend National Park in southwest Texas come stories of a five-foot-tall greenish-brown lizard that runs on two legs. Called the Mountain Boomer because it produces a bark like "distant thunder," this monster, described as a theropod dinosaur, lives in remote mountainous regions. However, a smaller local lizard that didn't die out in the Cretaceous period fits the same description, although it's not five feet tall.

Mountain Boomer is a term used for the eastern collared lizard, a fourteen-inch lizard that can run on two legs and looks like a tiny dinosaur. It's the state lizard of nearby Oklahoma.

Although the Mountain Boomer grows to just more than a foot tall, this hasn't stopped people from reportedly seeing ones that are the size of a man. In the 1970s, a Texan in the Big Bend area reported that his car had been run off the road by a theropod dinosaur, and in the early 1990s, a person claimed to encounter a similar dinosaur eating roadkill, but when the car approached, the dinosaur ran off.

UFO researcher Jimmy Ward wrote about the Mountain Boomer in an article by the same name. He interviewed a Connecticut family traveling through Texas that saw an enormous lizard with heavy back legs, and small front legs that looked like it came from the movie *Jurassic Park*.

Chupacabra

A list of Texas monsters wouldn't be complete without the Chupacabra. The legendary goatsucker (that's what the name means) was first seen in Puerto Rico in the 1990s and has spread into Mexico and the American Southwest. This hairless beast has needle-like fangs, large red eyes, a row of spines down its back, and is occasionally reported to have bat-like wings. The creature gets its name from the association between sightings and the death of small livestock that are drained of blood.

A myriad of reports have surfaced over the years of people capturing a Chupacabra on their property (a number of those reports are from Texas). DNA tests reveal that these creatures are really mangy dogs, coyotes, or raccoons.

Bigfoot

Tales of Bigfoot have graced almost every state in this book, so the big furry fellow only gets a cursory mention here. Although popular entertainment depicts the landscape of Texas to be far removed from the stereotypical Sasquatch haunts of the Pacific Northwest, it's not. East Texas is covered by thick pine forests and is a hotbed of Bigfoot sightings. Although East Texas has by far the most Bigfoot encounter reports in the state, sightings dot the entire map.

One place in Texas where people always see Bigfoot is the unincorporated community of Bigfoot southwest of San Antonio, population 450.

CHAPTER 44
UTAH

UTAH, THE CROSSROADS OF the West, became the forty-fifth of the United States in 1896. At 84,916 square miles, Utah is the thirteenth-largest state, but has one of the least dense populations. Early settlers to Utah include mountain men, adventurers, scientists, and Mormons persecuted for their religion. The headquarters of the Mormon Church, the Church of Jesus Christ of Latter-day Saints, is in Salt Lake City. The geography of Utah is 33 percent true desert, 40 percent steppes, 3 percent humid continental, and 24 percent mountainous. Of the numerous mountain ranges in Utah, the only mountain peaks taller than thirteen thousand feet are in the Uinta Mountains, and there are twenty-four. Utah's largest lake, the Great Salt Lake, has a length of 74.56 miles, an area of 1,699 square miles, and is the largest saltwater lake in the Western Hemisphere. Famous Utah residents include outlaw Robert Leroy Parker (otherwise known as Butch Cassidy), firearms designer John M. Browning, inventor of the television Philo T. Farnsworth, founder of Atari

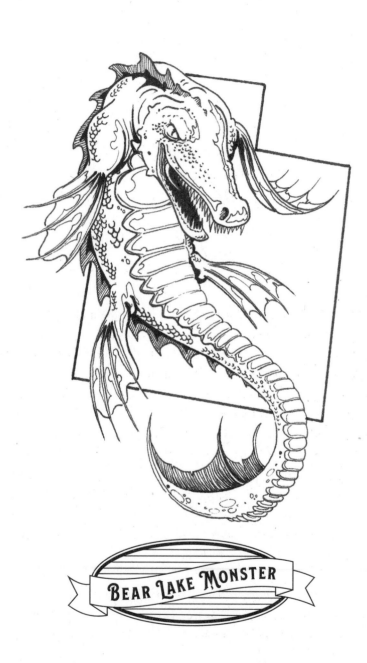

BEAR LAKE MONSTER

Games and the Chuck E. Cheese's Pizza-Time Theaters chain Nolan Bushnell, and inventor of the Zamboni machine Frank Zamboni. Utah also has strange things in its skies.

Flying Reptiles

Something unexpected and scaly apparently flew the skies of Utah in the late 1800s. In an edition of the 1894 *Ogden Standard-Examiner*, a group of "reliable men" saw what they described as a one-hundred-foot-long serpent flying over the town of Eden. The creature swooped down over the town by a park. The men believed the creature was flying between thirty-five and forty miles per hour. The monster soon disappeared into the mountains.

Although the residents of Eden never saw that flying reptile again, a number of people camping on Stansbury Island on the Great Salt Lake witnessed a creature they described as being a "combination of fish, alligator and bat," according a September 1903 edition of the *Pittsburgh (Pennsylvania) Press*. Witnesses claim the monster was at least fifty feet long; some swore it was at least sixty-five feet. The head was shaped like an alligator's with long "saw-edged teeth" in its gaping snout. The rest of the monster was covered in scales.

The creature flew toward the group on enormous bat-like wings, and when it grew close, it swung down over the crowd, and grabbed a horse in its mouth. The animal shot back into the air, and came to rest on a nearby mountain, from which the witnesses could hear it feeding off the horse. They fled the island in terror.

Bear Lake Monster

In July 1868, Joseph C. Rich, a correspondent for the *Deseret News*, wrote a letter to the editor that told the tale of a horrific beast that lived beneath the surface of Bear Lake. The lake itself is a freshwater lake that spans the border of Utah and Idaho. With a surface area of 109 square miles, a length of 18.33 miles, and an average depth of ninety-four feet, it's certainly big enough for a monster.

Rich's letter detailed an old Native American legend of a giant serpent that lived in the lake. It had short, squatty legs and often crawled onto shore searching for food, sometimes catching a man, woman, or child as they came to bathe in the lake.

The letter continued with the first report of a white settler encountering the monster, Mr. S.M. Johnson, who "saw something in the lake." Johnson thought the object was a drowned man, but when he approached the beach he saw it was no man. "Two or three feet of some kind of an animal that he had never seen before" broke the surface. The monster shot water from its nose, but didn't approach the beach. Johnson caught sight of a great bulk, which he assumed was the creature's body, just under the surface of the water.

Rich continued with another encounter by a man and three women who saw a large creature in the lake, swimming "much faster than a horse could run on land." Other encounters, he claimed in his letter, placed the Bear Lake Monster as being more than ninety feet long and traveling at a high rate of speed.

Unfortunately, Rich, a notorious prankster, eventually admitted to fabricating the stories. Or did he? Long after Rich passed on, people are still seeing the Bear Lake Monster.

In 2004, Bear Lake businessman Brian Hirschi told the *Deseret News* he'd seen the monster two years before but didn't tell anyone for fear of ridicule.

Hirschi claimed he was anchoring his pontoon boat at the end of the day when he saw "these two humps in the water." The humps were about one hundred yards away. He thought they were simply debris or lost water skis until they disappeared under the surface, and his boat began to rise.

"I started to get scared," Hirschi told the newspaper. "The next thing I know, a serpentlike creature shot up out of the water."

Hirschi described the monster as having "really dark, slimy green skin and deep beet-red eyes." The monster roared, then ducked back into the lake, and disappeared.

Great Salt Lake Whales

Sticking to the waters of Utah, legend has it that in June 1890, Englishman James Wickham imported to the Great Salt Lake two thirty-five-foot-long whales captured in the waters off Australia. The whales were brought to San Francisco and transported to Salt Lake City via rail. Wickham's plan was to release the whales into the lake where they would form a breeding population the locals could hunt for lamp oil.

The Provo *Utah Enquirer* carried the only known report on the whales. The newspaper claimed that once delivered to Utah and deposited into a pen constructed in the lake, the whales "suddenly made a beeline for deep water and shot through the wire fence as if it had been made of threads. In twenty minutes, they were out of sight and the chagrined Mr. Wickham stood gazing helplessly at the big salt water."

Six months after the whales disappeared, the *Enquirer* story went on, a representative of Wickham found the whales fifty miles from where they had been deposited "playing" in the water. The *Enquirer* (which no longer exists) claimed the pair reproduced and became a fixture of the lake.

That's where the story ends.

In 1995, the *Deseret News* tried to find evidence of the Great Salt Lake whales and came up dry. "If there actually were whales in the Great Salt Lake, just waiting to supply the oil lamps of pioneering Deseret Territory residents, no mention is made of them in any source the *Deseret News* could find," according to an article in the newspaper.

The University of Utah addresses the whales on the Department of Biology's web page: "Though there have been several alleged whale sightings, scientists believe that they could not have survived the lake's high salt content."

Giants

Tales abound of eight- to nine-foot-tall red-haired giants in the American West. Utah is no exception. According to an 1891 article in the *New York Sun*, the skeleton of an eight-foot-six-inch tall man was uncovered near the Jordan River near Salt Lake City. Workers clearing land for an irrigation ditch came upon the skull of the giant eight feet down. What was even more surprising to the workers is that the skeleton was standing upright. They had to dig down nine more feet to completely clear the remains.

The Sun claimed the skull to be "eleven inches in diameter and the feet nineteen inches long." Stone tools, pottery, and copper items were found in the area, although the most curious find was a necklace that held three copper medallions adorned with an undecipherable writing. The newspaper didn't reveal what happened to the skeleton or the artifacts.

Native American legends from the area tell of a race of red-haired giants in the mountains that grew to twelve feet in height. The giants were highly territorial, and would slay and devour anyone they found in their territory. Local tribes banded together, and chased these giant cannibals into a cave in the mountains. When the giants refused to come out of the cave, the warriors filled the entrance with wood and set it on fire, filling the cavern with smoke and killing the monsters.

Bigfoot

Given that there are eighty mountain ranges in Utah to hold a lot of mysteries, the state was bound to have stories of Bigfoot. A 1977 article in the *Standard-Examiner* details one such report from high in the Uinta Mountains.

A group of hikers from North Ogden saw a ten-foot-tall "gorilla" covered in a "mantle" of white hair over its shoulders that tapered to dark hair on the lower parts of its large, thick body. The creature walked on two legs.

According to the newspaper, hunter Jay Barker and his two sons hiked to the top of a ridge where they met Larry Beeson and his three sons. The group then saw a creature standing by a lake at the bottom of the ridge. They initially thought the animal was an elk. When one of the boys accidentally dislodged some rocks that rolled downhill, the creature stood and looked up at them.

"What are we looking at?" Beeson told the newspaper.

The creature walked away but kept its attention on the group as it walked into the trees. After it disappeared into the timber, the group went down to the lake and discovered gigantic footprints.

CHAPTER 45
VERMONT

VERMONT IS SMALL. AT 9,616 square miles, the entire state could be dropped into Africa's Lake Victoria. According to US Census data, Vermont is the second least populous state (behind Wyoming) with 626,042 residents. It is bordered by New York, Massachusetts, New Hampshire, and the Canadian province of Quebec. There are mountains in Vermont, along with forests. What Vermont lacks in human population, it makes up for in trees. The state is 78 percent woodland with 4.46 million acres of forest. The state's firsts include the first state to join the original thirteen colonies and the first state to abolish slavery; it's also first on the list of maple syrup producing states, making 40.7 percent of the country's favorite pancake topping. Famous residents include President Calvin Coolidge, Mormon leaders Joseph Smith and Brigham Young, blacksmith and plow manufacturer John Deere, inventor of the DC electric motor Thomas Davenport, and inventor of the modern elevator Elisha Otis. Vermont is also fond of its pigs. No, wait. Its Pigman.

AWFUL

Northfield Pigman

As legend has it, the night before Halloween in 1951, a teenager named Sam Harris left home with rolls of toilet paper and a basket of eggs to create holiday trouble. Harris never returned. His parents phoned the authorities, and search parties combed the area, but he was never found.

Here the legend follows two paths.

The first story tells that Sam gave himself to the devil, devouring the raw entrails of a pig, and wearing the head over his own. Soon after, unexplained animal deaths were blamed on the Pigman. This story has Sam coming to his mother's house three years later, depositing the disemboweled organs of a pig on the family porch before squealing like a pig himself and running into the surrounding forest.

The second story, however, is only slightly less disturbing—the Pigman may have eaten Harris.

Whichever the case, the Pigman did not go away.

Years after Harris's disappearance, high school students left a dance to drink beer in a sandpit near the school when a monster came out of the woods. It walked like a man, but was covered in white fur, and had a pig's face. As it lurched toward them, the terrified teenagers dropped their beer and rushed back to the dance. No one believed them. Some of the braver students went out to search the sandpit, and although there was no monster, the nearby grass had been trampled by something large.

Then Pigman sightings began coming in from all over the area around Northfield. Farmers reported seeing the monster on their property, drivers said it ran across the road in front of their cars, teens making out in an area filled with waterfalls and caves called the Devil's Washbowl said it banged on their car windows. People reported finding bones and cloven hoof prints in one cave of the Washbowl, and that brought people to hunt for the Pigman.

Although the Pigman was never captured, it's a popular story to tell in the wilds of Vermont in the dark.

The Awful

With what may be the greatest monster name ever, the Awful is a griffin-like creature first seen by two sawmill workers in the early 1900s in the town of Richford near the Canadian border. The men were crossing the Main Street bridge when they saw the beast glaring at them from the nearby rooftop of the Boright building. It had gray skin, a long, serpentlike tail, a twenty-foot wingspan, and "huge claws that could easily grip a milk can's girth."

Although no one knew what the monster was, or where it came from, local residents knew it wasn't leaving any time soon. Farmers reported it flying over their fields. Terrified residents cowered in their homes as the beast landed on their rooftops. The people who witnessed the Awful said it seemed to simply watch them. A farm wife named Oella Hopkins was hanging up the wash outside when her dog began to bark. When she looked to see what was troubling it, she found the Awful sitting on her rooftop, glaring at her. She ran inside and hid beneath her bed for hours.

The Awful gained such a reputation that in 1925 the famous horror and science fiction author H.P. Lovecraft visited the towns of Richford and Berkshire from his native Rhode Island to find out more about the monster. Lovecraft wrote, "The Awful became ample sustenance for my imagination."

Sightings of the Awful all but stopped after the 1920s, although they resumed in 2006. According to an article in the nearby Enosburg Falls *County Courier*, an anonymous eyewitness claimed to have seen "an unbelievable looking winged monster... What I saw was no yarn. Yarns don't fly and stories don't look like that. What I saw was real. And I hope to high heaven I never see it again."

Memphre

Lake Memphremagog is a nearly forty-square-mile glacial lake that stretches between Newport, Vermont, and Magog, Quebec. It has an average depth of 51 feet, but its maximum depth of 351 may be deep enough to hide a monster known as Memphre.

The stories of Memphre go back a long way. When European settlers reached this region, the local Indians warned them away from the lake and its serpent. According to an article written by Memphre researcher Jacques Boisvert, who died in February 2006, the monster made many appearances in the early local press. "One of the first sightings which dates back to January 21, 1847, came from the *Stanstead Journal*. Here is an extract: 'I am not aware whether it is generally known that a strange animal something of a sea serpent... exists in lake Memphremagog.'" Articles on sightings of this creature stretch throughout the 1800s.

Barbara Malloy of the Memphremagog Historical Society of Newport has seen the monster herself and described it to the *Huffington Post*. "When I first saw it... I thought it was jet skiers because it was moving fast," she said. "But when it turned to go south more it was parallel to the road and I could see from the side view that it had a head like a horse, a long neck, and a big body. As it got closer I could see that it was pretty tall and as long as a house." The creature eventually turned, and disappeared from view into a growing mist.

Malloy's encounter isn't the only modern-day sighting of the creature. By the time of his death, Boisvert had collected nearly 230 sightings of the Lake Memphremagog serpent.

Willy

Willoughby, a 2.636-square-mile lake with a maximum depth of three hundred feet, rests roughly twenty miles southeast of Lake Memphremagog, and is home to its own monster tales. Stories of the Willoughby Lake monster known as Willy stretch back to the 1800s. A report of a monster in the lake appeared in an 1868 edition of the nearby Caledonia newspaper: "It is reported that the great water snake at Willoughby Lake was killed Wednesday of last week by Stephen Edmonds of Newport, VT." The articles says a twelve-year-old boy sliced the beast in half with a sickle. It was twenty-three feet long.

The article doesn't speculate what the monster was, although modern-day researchers suspect it was an eel. In the 1950s, navy divers looking for the body of a fellow sailor who drowned while on leave apparently saw eels at the bottom of the lake; they estimated the eels were eight feet long. However, the longest freshwater eel on record tops out at around seven feet long.

New Jersey resident Audrey Besse reported seeing Willy while visiting Vermont in the mid-1980s. Besse, her mother, and a friend were sitting near a beach when they saw "a long, dark, creature with two or three humps in the middle of the lake, swimming toward the south end." Besse went to fetch her camera, but the monster was gone before she could take a picture.

Champ

Lake Champlain, a 490-square-mile, four-hundred-foot-deep freshwater lake, is mostly in New York State but also goes into Canada and Vermont. Champlain is the swimming hole of Champ, America's most famous lake monster.

Like at Lake Memphremagog, Native Americans warned early white settlers of the monster. The first newspaper account was from July 1819, when Captain Crum of the ship *Bulwagga Bay* saw a black monster that stretched 187 feet long, according to the *Plattsburgh Republican*. The monster had a head like a sea horse, which stuck about fifteen feet from the water.

A railroad crew saw a gigantic serpent with silvery scales in the lake in 1873. A county sheriff saw a thirty-foot-long "water serpent" in the lake that July, and in August, a steamship collided with a water monster and almost overturned.

Champ sightings continue to this day.

Bigfoot

Although every state but Hawaii claims Bigfoot as its hairiest resident, not every state has photographic evidence. In 2010, Vermont Bigfoot researcher Frank Siecienski claimed to have just that. When Siecienski and his wife noticed apples disappearing from a tree in the yard of their Hubbardton home, he put out a trail camera to capture the thief.

The first pictures only yielded a coyote. A subsequent photograph, however, revealed something bigger.

"Both my wife and I, at the exact same time, said, 'My god, what in the world is that?'" Siecienski told NBC5 of Burlington and Plattsburgh, New York.

The photograph shows a hairy, possibly bipedal animal crouched in the Siecienskis' yard. Although this photograph has given Siecienski international attention, at least some people back home don't think the subject is that unusual. When Siecienski took his picture to a biologist, the scientist disregarded it. "He said it was an owl. But I don't think owls grow to five hundred pounds," Siecienski told WCAX in Burlington, Vermont.

CHAPTER 46
VIRGINIA

THE COMMONWEALTH OF VIRGINIA began in 1607 as the Colony of Virginia, the first permanent British settlement in the New World. It was also one of the original thirteen colonies to declare its independence from England. Virginia's General Assembly is the oldest law-making group in the New World. Virginia was also the capital of the Confederate States of America during the American Civil War. Virginia and Maryland donated the land that became Washington, DC, and because of that proximity to the nation's capital about one-fourth of Virginia workers are employed by the United States government. Virginia's geography includes the Appalachian Plateau, the Blue Ridge Mountains, and coastal plains; the easternmost part of the state is bordered by Chesapeake Bay and the Atlantic Ocean. And there are trees, lots and lots of trees. Sixty-two percent of the state is forested, which makes up about 15.7 million acres. Famous residents include Pocahontas (a Native American who helped the first British colonists in Virginia), civil rights activist Booker T.

WEREWOLF

Washington, screenwriter and *Breaking Bad* creator Vince Gilligan, jazz singer Ella Fitzgerald, explorer Richard Byrd, and eight United States presidents, including George Washington. It's also home to the Bunny Man.

Bunny Man

US Air Force Academy cadet Robert Bennett and his fiancée were driving home from a football game around midnight October 19, 1970, when they parked in a field off Guinea Road in Burke, a town near Washington, DC. Bennett was going to see if a relative was still awake, but they never got out of the car. As they sat with the motor running, something smashed into the front passenger window, showering them with glass. When they looked, a person dressed in a white bunny suit stood outside the shattered window and shouted, "You're on private property and I have your tag number," according to a 1970 article in the *Washington Post*. Bennett gunned the engine and sped away. The couple later discovered a strange hatchet inside the car, which they gave to police as evidence of the event.

The Bunny Man was just getting started. Ten days after the Bennett attack, Paul Phillips, a security guard on a construction site, saw a man dressed in a gray and white bunny costume standing on the porch of a house under construction near Guinea Road. Phillips described the man as being in his early twenties, about five feet, eight inches tall, and 175 pounds, according to a paper by historian-archivist Brian A. Conley of the Fairfax County Public Library. When Phillips approached, the Bunny Man started chopping at the porch with an axe, telling the guard, "All you people trespass around here. If you don't get out of here, I'm going to bust you on the head."

Police investigated the Bennett and Phillips accounts but were baffled. They were even more baffled at all the following reports—more than fifty people saw the Bunny Man that year. Sightings allegedly continue, sometimes as far away as Maryland, but mostly around what has been dubbed Bunny Man Bridge in Virginia. As legend has it, the Bunny Man preys on drinking teenagers who hang out near the bridge, although evidence of anything really happening is nonexistent. The legend claims the Bunny Man escaped from an insane asylum in 1904. Take that for what it's worth.

Giant Birds

Enormous birds have a place in many Native American legends. With wingspans of greater than twenty feet, the Thunderbird is larger than any avian that has existed for ten thousand years. This is when the Teratorn flew the skies of North America. However, according to eyewitnesses, these enormous prehistoric birds may still be seen in the skies of Virginia today.

In 2013, in New Kent County, a witness reported seeing an enormous bird standing in the middle of the highway. As the witness pulled around a corner, the bird stood in the center of the road—it was taller than the witness's car, and its wings stretched across the highway. The vehicle startled the bird, and it took off, the flapping of its wings almost deafening.

Birds of this size have been reported in New York, Pennsylvania, Ohio, Texas, and New Mexico.

Werewolf

A resident of a Woodbridge neighborhood saw something unexpected one night in mid-October 2011—a canine they couldn't identify. "A coyote, or a werewolf," Prince William County police spokesman Jonathan Perok told InsideNoVa.com. The witness saw the creature lurking in the woods near a shopping center just after 10:00 p.m. Police were dispatched to the area, but no trace of the mythical creature was found.

In nearby Henrico County, mostly around the Confederate Hills Recreation Center, werewolf sightings are more common. A doglike creature at least six feet tall and covered in gray fur has been seen running on four legs, and sometimes two legs, through the woods. Although there are no records of deaths associated with the wolf man, it has been known to chase people. Howls are reported around the time of the full moon.

More reports have come from southern Virginia near the Great Dismal Swamp. An eight-year-old boy reported rolling over in bed one night, and looked out his window only to come face-to-face with a monster. The creature, he claimed, had to be standing on its hind legs to be looking into the window. It had a humanlike face—except for the nose, which was a snout like a dog's. The beast stared at him with yellow eyes. The boy shot out of bed and spent the rest of the night sleeping in his mother's room.

Snallygaster

As far back as the 1700s, Virginia residents claimed a giant reptilian bird would appear in the sky and swoop down to attack pets, game, livestock, and sometimes children. Eyewitness descriptions of the Snallygaster sound like that of a pterosaur: an enormous flying monster with a wingspan of twenty-five to thirty feet, a long beak, and leathery skin that looks like a reptile's. However, the Snallygaster also has tentacles, talons of steel, and carries with it the pungent scent of death. Its shriek resembles a train whistle.

Reports of the Snallygaster continued until the 1930s when they became sporadic, appearing again in 1948 and 1973.

Bigfoot

Seeing as how Bigfoot has been reported in every state but Hawaii, it's expected there would be Bigfoot sightings in Virginia. In 2014, a Virginia man not only had an encounter with the big furry hominid, he photographed it on the Intracoastal Waterway.

Randy O'Neal was fishing with his father and a friend when they saw the creature and took a picture O'Neal was impressed with, according to WTVR. "Finally, a photo that is not blurry nor hidden behind a tree. A clear photo of Bigfoot standing out in the wide open. You be the judge," O'Neal posted on YouTube.

It may be a tree stump.

CHAPTER 47
WASHINGTON

WASHINGTON STATE, THE MOST northwestern of the contiguous United States, is bordered on the north by Canada, the south by Oregon, and the east by Idaho. It is the eighteenth largest of the United States, and has the thirteenth-largest population, although most of that population lives in and around the city of Seattle. The geography of Washington is diverse; there are lowlands, fjords, rivers, glaciers, and mountains (which include several volcanoes). The varying landscapes have one thing in common—trees. An estimated 40.7 percent of the state is covered in them. Famous Washingtonians include game show host Bob Barker, Nirvana front man Kurt Cobain, Microsoft founder Bill Gates, guitarist Jimi Hendrix, and TV's Batman, Adam West. Washington state is the only state to be named after a president. It's also the only state with a Batsquatch.

BIGFOOT

Batsquatch

Mt. Saint Helens (slogan, "come for the scenery, stay for the terrifying cryptids and magma") is an active volcano in the Cascade Mountains that boasts a VolcanoCam, Zipline Adventure, and gift shop. The volcano erupted in May 1980, producing avalanches that could have filled one million Olympic-sized swimming pools with debris. Around that time, Mt. Saint Helens also produced the Batsquatch.

After the eruption, people around the mountain began to report seeing a nine-foot-tall bluish-purple ape with blazing yellow eyes, and enormous bat wings.

The *Tacoma News Tribune* carried an article in April 1994 about eighteen-year-old Brian Canfield's encounter with the monster. While driving along the edge of a forest, Canfield's pickup unexpectedly shut down, and crawled to a stop. According to the article, "He saw the feet, descending. Bird feet. Claw feet. Then the legs, the torso, the chest. And the wings, folded, attached to the back of the broad shoulders. Then the head. That face. The creature, nine feet tall. Thirty feet away. Blue-tinted fur, yellowish eyes, tufted ears and sharp straight teeth. With a dust-raising thud it landed." The monster glared at Canfield for a while, how long he didn't know. Then it spread its wings and took off. With the beast gone, the truck started, and Canfield sped home.

In 2009, two friends hiking around Mount Shasta saw a "Hulk Hogan"-sized ape with "leathery wings" fly from a crevice and disappear into a grove of trees.

In 2011, a Washington man walking his dog saw something large in the sky with "bat wings, blue fur and…eyes glowing red. It was about nine feet tall at the least, after I watched it just flew away."

Cadborosaurus

Lurking in the waters off the coast of Washington is a horse-headed serpent that has been seen up and down the coast of the Pacific Northwest for centuries. Although common in Native American folklore, the first sighting of this creature, the Cadborosaurus, by Europeans dates back to the 1700s. The Cadborosaurus is described as a fifty-foot-long grayish-brown serpent with vertical coils and flippers.

There have been hundreds of sightings throughout the Pacific Northwest since the early 1900s, such as the 1934 report of thirty-foot-long remains discovered on Washington's Henry Island. Whalers just north of Washington in Canadian waters found a Cadborosaurus in the belly of a sperm whale. In 1963, a rotting corpse with a horselike head was found on the shores of Washington's Oak Harbor.

In 2009, a fisherman named Kelly Nash shot a video in Alaska of what he claims to be a Cadborosaurus.

Basket Ogress

Indigenous peoples of the American Northwest up into Canada—the Tlingit, Kwakiutl, Heiltsuk, and Salish—all have a similar story of the Basket Ogress.

The Basket Ogress is an angry, hungry giant who carries a huge basket with her to scoop up naughty children who stray too far from home. She takes the children back to her lair to cook over hot coals or boil in a pot.

The Basket Ogress's main weakness is her stupidity. Most of her victims seem to escape.

Stories of the Basket Ogress are used mainly as these tribes' bogeyman.

Drunken Bears

Bears are dangerous. There are an estimated twenty-five thousand black bears in Washington—that's eleven times more bears in the state than Italian immigrants. The bears are also apparently thirsty.

In 2004, campers at Baker Lake woke to find a black bear lying unconscious outside their tent amongst a littering of empty beer cans. During the night the bear opened the cooler and got into the beer. Campers had two brands in the cooler, the national domestic brand Busch and the popular regional brand Rainier. The bear apparently preferred Rainier—it drank thirty-six of them. "He drank the Rainier and wouldn't drink the Busch beer," campground bookkeeper Lisa Broxson told NBC News.

Wildlife agents tried to remove the bear, but it climbed into a tree because it simply wanted to sleep. Four hours later, agents chased the bear away; however, it came back to the spot the next morning. Agents brought in a humane trap and baited it with honey, doughnuts, and two open cans of Rainier. That did the trick. After trapping the bear, authorities relocated it away from the campground.

A Whole Bunch of Bigfoot

The Pacific Northwest is built for three things: logging, fishing, and Bigfoot. Washington has recorded more Bigfoot encounters than any other state, with 573, according to the *Philadelphia Inquirer*. The first instance of Bigfoot reported by white settlers in Washington is from a letter written in April 1840 by Protestant missionary Rev. Elkanah Walker. Walker wrote that the local Native Americans spoke of a "race of giants which inhabit a certain mountain off to the west of us." The giants, covered in hair, would come down from the mountain and steal the tribe's salmon.

With 573 reports, sightings have obviously continued.

In July 2000, David Mills, a forest manager with the Suquamish Indian tribe, was inspecting the health of young trees when he heard strange sounds from deeper in the forest. He soon discovered what was making the noise.

"I watched this hairy thing on two legs," he said in an article in the British Columbia, Canada, newspaper the *Province*. "It used its left arm to lift up a branch ... He turned in my direction and saw I was watching him, and ducked behind a tree." The creature was covered in black hair and was at least nine feet tall.

Fascinated, Mills tried to get closer to the beast, but it didn't want that. The Bigfoot began to scream and pound a tree with a rock. The closer Mills got, the louder the Bigfoot's protest. But soon Mills discovered maybe it wasn't him the Bigfoot was trying to warn away. A mother bear and cub came out of the brush to Mills's left (no word if the mother bear was intoxicated).

A Bigfoot and two bears? Mills had enough. He turned and ran. "I flew down that hill," he told the paper. "Then I just hopped in my truck and locked up the gate, and left the area."

When Mills returned to the spot much later, he found a Bigfoot print, 15.7 inches long, and eight inches wide.

And that's just one story of Washington's Bigfoot. There are 572 more.

Rock Lake Monster

Rock Lake, near the Idaho border, is a seven-mile-long, mile-wide sliver of water that, at 375-feet deep, may be the home of a legendary serpent.

Native Americans held Rock Lake as taboo after a monster rose from the depths of the lake hundreds of years ago and devoured an entire tribe. Although there are no clear descriptions of this creature, it is often described as shaped like a swimming log that disappears under the water. Sightings are rare, but they do occur.

A 1995 article in the *Spokesman-Review* quoted a local amateur historian on sightings of the monster.

"My sis owns property on one of the lake's points," the historian told the newspaper. He asked to remain anonymous. "One evening, she was rounding the point into a bay when she saw something huge on top of the water suddenly splash and go under. I asked her how big it was. 'It was as big as a tree and stretched further across than my living room,' she said. I think it was a sturgeon myself."

Sturgeon seems to be the popular answer for the surface sightings, as well as for the enormous underwater moving objects fishermen have seen with electronic equipment. The largest sturgeons can grow up to eighteen feet long and weigh up to 4,400 pounds, which is pretty monstrous. However, according to the Washington Department of Fish and Wildlife, there are no sturgeons in Rock Lake.

CHAPTER 48
WEST VIRGINIA

WEST VIRGINIA HAS ALWAYS been a rebel. During the American Civil War, fifty counties of the Confederate state Virginia split off to form their own state: West Virginia. This was the only state admitted to the Union during the war and is the only state to have separated from a Confederate state. The Appalachian Mountains make up two-thirds of West Virginia, covering most of its 24,230 square miles in forested peaks and valleys. Bordered by the northern states of Ohio and Pennsylvania, and the southern states of Virginia and Kentucky, West Virginia is simultaneously considered the northernmost Southern state, and the southernmost Northern state. It's the ninth-smallest state and has the twelfth-smallest population, but West Virginia is scrappy. The state is known for coal mining and logging, as well as outdoor recreation like white-water rafting and mountain biking. West Virginia is home to the first Mother's Day (1908) and the first federal women's penitentiary (1926). Famous West Virginians include actor Don Knotts, Air Force test pilot Chuck

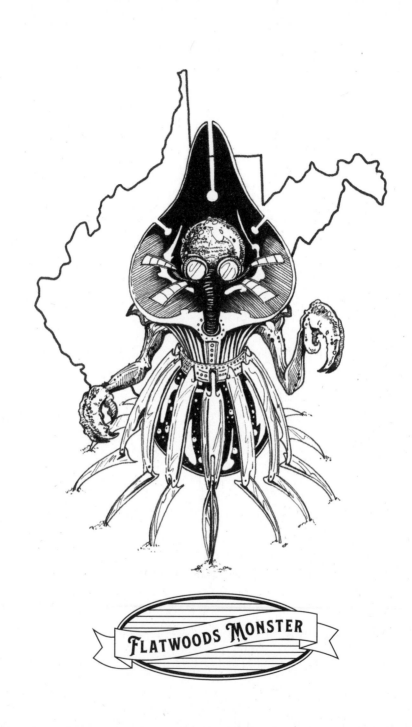

Yeager (the man who broke the sound barrier), author Pearl Buck, and Olympic gold medal gymnast Mary Lou Retton. It's also home to Mothman.

Mothman

A week starting on November 12, 1966, was busy in an area of western West Virginia near the Ohio border. Gravediggers near the small town of Clendenin reported that a winged, man-sized creature swooped low over their heads. Three days later, Roger and Linda Scarberry and Steve and Mary Mallette of nearby Point Pleasant were parking at the TNT area (a three-thousand-acre swatch of forests, wetland, and farms that is home to an abandoned World War II munitions factory outside town) when they saw something that would haunt them for years. Their car headlights shone on a tall, black, manlike figure with glowing red eyes. As they sped away from the area, the creature opened its wings and flew after them, its wingspan wider than the car. Steve Mallette told the *Point Pleasant Register* the creature "was like a man with wings...It wasn't anything like you'd seen on TV or in a monster movie."

Over the next year the creature was seen by more than one hundred people, including volunteer firefighters, in the area around Point Pleasant. Police and wildlife officials blamed the sightings on a rogue heron or sandhill crane. Then a dog disappeared, and strange sounds began to come from people's televisions sets. But when the Silver Bridge, connecting Point Pleasant with Gallipolis, Ohio, collapsed during rush hour on December 15, 1967, killing forty-six people, locals began to blame the Mothman for all their troubles.

Although the most notable sightings occurred in the late 1960s, Mothman (named by a newspaper reporter in the 1960s who was a fan of the cartoonish *Batman* TV series) reports continue today across multiple states and countries. The most recent sighting was a 2016 report by an anonymous man driving on Route 2 in Virginia. A picture the man took was televised by WCHS-TV.

Sheepsquatch

The TNT area isn't just the stomping ground of a black, man-sized terror. It's also the home to a white, man-sized terror—the Sheepsquatch. This beast is a bipedal creature covered in white wool with a pointed head, a fang-filled mouth, and the horns of a goat. In an interview with *Modern Farmer* magazine, Kurt McCoy, author of *White Things: West Virginia's Weird White Monsters*, said, "The TNT area itself is just chock full of amazing weirdness."

The weirdness began in the 1990s when a hunter saw a white, manlike, goat-headed beast break from a line of brush and stop to drink at a creek. Not noticing the man, it casually rose and continued through the forest.

Not long after the hunter's sighting, a family returning from a reunion saw a tall goatlike creature step from the woods. "The witnesses described it as being seven to eight feet tall, covered in shaggy white hair with legs like a man," McCoy told *Modern Farmer*. "And they described the face as looking a bit long like a sheep and having horns like a ram's."

That same decade, the monster was seen by children who claimed a white, horned bear on two feet watched them play in their yard; a motorist saw it sitting in a ditch; and campers claim the Sheepsquatch threatened them at their campsite in the evening, but wouldn't approach the fire.

Flatwoods Monster

Not all West Virginia's monsters come from the TNT area; some come from space.

Three boys saw a bright light streak across the sky on September 12, 1952. When the light landed on a local farm, the children alerted adults, who took everyone to see what it was. When the group arrived, they found a ball of "fire" atop a hill, surrounded by a mist that irritated their eyes and burned their nostrils. One member of the group shouted and pointed toward two lights that loomed over the object. Flashlight beams shot toward the lights and struck a black creature at least seven feet tall with a head the shape of a "sideways diamond." A cowl shaped like the ace of spades sat behind the creature's head; its eyes glowed green. Then the creature hissed and moved toward the group, which sent them running.

They alerted the sheriff's department and the local newspaper. Although deputies and the reporter scoured the area, they found nothing that night. The next morning, however, the reporter discovered prints and a strange black liquid at the sight of the alleged encounter.

Reports of encounters began to come in from all over the county, and the creature began to take another form. Witnesses described it as looking more like a mechanical device than a flesh-and-blood monster. Flying saucers, strange odors, and electronic disruptions were common during these sightings. Although the encounters were dynamic, they were brief, and the Flatwoods Monster vanished from West Virginia as quickly as it had come.

Ogua

Legend has it a river monster the size of a bear but shaped like a turtle lurks in the Monongahela River in the northern part of West Virginia. Early European settlers to the area said the creature, the two-headed Ogua, lived beneath the river waters by day, but at night would come to the banks to feast on deer, striking the unsuspecting animals with its long, deadly tail and dragging them into the water to feed.

Early stories tell of encounters with the creature, including the troubles of a family that lived alongside the Monongahela River in the mid-1700s. While fishing, an enormous turtle emerged from the water and snatched a twelve-year-old boy from the shore. The family searched for the child, but he was never found. Days later, the family was awakened by the sound of a large animal rubbing against their cabin. One of the children dared a look and saw a huge, dark, turtle-shaped bulk outside the home. The family moved soon after.

Appalachian Black Panther

Black panthers exist. Big cats that are usually spotted, such as jaguars, leopards, and bobcats, can be melanistic. This is when a greater than normal amount of dark pigment makes an animal appear black. The bobcat, though, isn't large enough to account for the puma-sized big cat seen in the mountains of West Virginia; leopards are native to Africa and Asia; and the jaguar is native to Central and South America (once native to the southern states, they are still reported in Texas and New Mexico; however sightings are quite rare). The black cats seen in West Virginia resemble black mountain lions, something our current science says doesn't exist.

However, black panthers were reported in West Virginia as far back as the first European settlers, and were taken seriously by science. An 1843 book by Sir William Jardine, *The Naturalist's Library, Mammalia, Vol. 1, Cats*, featured a great cat named *Felis Nigra*—the black puma. The listing included a watercolor drawing of the feline by James Hope Stewart. Two of the beasts were supposedly displayed in London in the 1700s, although there is no record of what happened to the cats.

Although still reported to this day, the Appalachian black panther falls into the realm of cryptozoology.

Stone Man

Every state but one has its story of Bigfoot. In West Virginia, it's the legend of the Stone Man.

Early European settlers to the area encountered enormous apes that would throw rocks at their camps, and later, their houses. The local Cherokee Indians called the tall humanlike creatures Nun'Yunu'Wi, which means "Stone Man" because no weapon could pierce its skin. Adventurers and later timbermen encountered the Stone Man much more often than they would have liked. Apparently, people still are encountering the Stone Man in West Virginia, to the tune of one hundred reports per year.

Like this report investigated by the Bigfoot Field Research Organization: In 2009, a timber worker was cutting down a tree when he noticed a black figure standing farther back in the forest. Although he first through it was a bear standing on its hind legs, the creature raised its left arm to lean against a tree. After a few minutes, it turned and walked into the forest like a human. The timberman saw the creature a year later, squatting over a puddle, scooping up water in its hand to drink.

CHAPTER 49
WISCONSIN

WISCONSIN, AMERICA'S DAIRYLAND, IS a state in the Upper Midwest bordered by Iowa, Illinois, Minnesota, the Upper Peninsula of Michigan, and two of the Great Lakes, Superior and Michigan. It's called America's Dairyland for a reason. The state of Wisconsin produces more than 3.5 billion gallons of milk per year, which is equivalent to the milk production of the United Kingdom. It also produces cheese, lots and lots of cheese, more than three billion pounds per year. Fans of Wisconsin's National Football League team the Green Bay Packers are affectionately called "cheeseheads." In terms of size and population, Wisconsin hovers around the middle of the United States for both. It's the twenty-third-largest state with the twentieth-largest population. The state is composed of plains and hills covered with farms. There are forests, though, a lot of them; roughly sixteen million acres that cover 46 percent of the state.

HODAG

Famous people from Wisconsin include inventor John Bardeen, the only person to win the Nobel Prize in Physics twice; magician Harry Houdini (born in Hungary, but lived his early life in Wisconsin); pianist Liberace; musician Les Paul, who invented the solid body electric guitar; producer/actor/director Orson Welles; painter Georgia O'Keeffe; circus owners Charles and John Ringling; author Laura Ingalls Wilder; and architect Frank Lloyd Wright. And more than its fair share of monsters.

Werewolves

Although werewolves in Wisconsin may seem out of place, or even a bit silly (go ahead, say it three times and see if you don't giggle), looking at it from a historical perspective it begins to make sense.

Some of the first Europeans to settle this lush state in the mid-1800s were Germans, and Germany has a long and deep tradition of these manlike, wolfish beasts. Quick to follow the Germans to Wisconsin were Scandinavians, Belgians, Dutch, Swiss, and the Irish—most of these cultures tell tales of werewolves. When people settle in different parts of the world, they bring with them their language, traditions, stories, and their monsters. Of course, the Native Americans of the area had similar monsters.

Werewolf sightings in Wisconsin were first cataloged in print in the 1930s.

A man driving in Jefferson County saw a man digging in a field. The driver slowed to watch the man when the figure stood to its full height and stared at him. It was not a man. The driver claimed the manlike creature was covered in hair and looked like a cross between a dog and an ape. The driver got a good enough look at the monster to see that its hands were shaped like human hands.

Similar stories of a man-wolf dot Wisconsin's history. In 1964, another driver saw the same monster run across the road in front of his car. The encounter was in the same county. The creature was tall, covered in brown hair, and ran like a man, but its head looked like a dog's. The wolf man sprinted in front of the man's car, leapt a fence, and vanished into a field.

The monster continued to stalk rural Wisconsin throughout the 1970s, but it wasn't until 1989 that the sightings escalated, this time near the town of Elkhorn, just south of Jefferson County.

Much like the previous encounters, Lorianne Endrizzi saw a dark figure that she mistook for a person on the side of the road. When she drove closer she saw it was a tall, hairy monster with the face of a dog, with prominent fangs and glowing yellow eyes. A local dairy farmer also saw the creature on his property that year, as did another driver on nearby Bray Road, and an eleven-year-old girl saw a dog walking on two legs across her family's property near that road.

Similar sightings continued through the 1990s, but it wasn't until 1999 that the beast made national news.

On Halloween night, Doristine Gipson, age eighteen, drove down Bray Road and hit something with her car. When she got out to check, she saw that she'd hit a werewolf—and it was not happy. The huge, shaggy creature bolted toward her. She dove back into her car and sped away. The werewolf jumped onto the vehicle but could not hold on. Gipson reported the incident to the police, who then told local reporter Linda Godfrey, who covered the incident. Godfrey has gone on to write books about these werewolf encounters including *The Beast of Bray Road: Tailing Wisconsin's Werewolf.*

Lake Koshkonong Monster

Jefferson County is apparently a monstrous place. It's not only home to numerous werewolf sightings, it's also home to the Lake Koshkonong monster.

Although this 10,595-acre lake is a natural body of water, the Indianford Dam on Rock River turned it into one of the state's larger lakes. Even so, it's only seven feet deep at its deepest. Fishermen come to the lake for bass, northern pike, catfish, and walleye, but sometimes they come for the monster.

According to a November 1887 article in the *Watertown Republican*, duck hunters A.I. Sherman of Fort Atkinson and Charles Bartlett of Milwaukee were rowing in a bay in the northeastern part of the lake when they saw an enormous serpent swimming about 150 feet from their boat. The creature stuck its head above water on a neck at least ten feet long and eight inches thick. The two estimated the beast to be at least forty feet long.

This is where the story gets weird. The duck hunters, instead of rowing as fast as they could away from a large, unknown animal, rowed forward trying to kill it. Before they could reach it, the Lake Koshkonong Monster slipped under the water and disappeared.

Jenny

Geneva Lake, a 7.5-mile-long, 144-feet-deep body of water in southeastern Wisconsin, is home to a monster similar to the Lake Koshkonong Monster. Locals call her Jenny.

According to the *Chicago Tribune*, the first recorded sighting of Jenny was in July 1892, when two boys saw an enormous snake while they were fishing. It was one hundred feet long and three feet thick. The creature burst from the water thirty yards away from the boys and started swimming toward them. The creature then turned back toward the deeper parts of the lake and dove under.

People from the town of Lake Geneva, which is on the shores of Geneva Lake, reported seeing Jenny numerous times by 1902, although sightings are now rare.

Creatures similar to Jenny and the Lake Koshkonong Monster have been reported in Devil's Lake, Pewaukee Lake, Lake Mendota, and Rock Lake.

Goatman of Hogsback Road

Hogsback Road is a short stretch of pavement near Hubertus. According to locals, the drive is dangerous, but maybe not so dangerous as Hogsback Road's most famous resident—the Goatman.

Witnesses have described this creature as a satyr from Greek mythology—a horned man with the lower body of a goat. This entity has appeared in the folklore of this area of rural Wisconsin since the late 1800s. However, unlike lake monsters, there are recent sightings, such as a 2003 encounter when two men saw what looked like a two-legged goat walk across the road in front of their car. The creature was the size of a man with large, muscular legs and tiny arms.

Mineral Point Vampire

A lanky, white-faced apparition dressed in a cape terrorized the area around Mineral Point from 1981 to 2008. Although the vampire never attacked anyone, his appearance made the locals nervous.

The first sighting of the vampire occurred when police were called to Graceland Cemetery in Mineral Point to investigate a trespassing. Officers found a dark figure lurking amongst the tombstones and attempted to approach it. This figure evaded them, easily climbed a fence and escaped. This was the first of many cemetery encounters between police and the "vampire."

In March 2008, police received numerous calls about a man in a tree. When they arrived at the tree, the Mineral Point vampire leapt to the ground, easily climbed a ten-foot-high concrete wall, and disappeared into the night.

The last encounter was in July 2008, when a young couple went fishing at night on a dock at Ludden Lake. In the silence of the night they caught the sound of something climbing below the planks where they sat. When the boyfriend stood and stomped on the dock, something splashed into the water. Nervous, he began to shine his flashlight toward the splashing to find a tall, thin man with a white face and black hair dressed in a cape climbing onto the dock. The young man threw his flashlight at the figure, and the couple rushed to their car. As they sped away, the girlfriend witnessed the Mineral Point vampire running toward them.

Trolls and Gnomes

The Devil's Punch Bowl near Menomonie was carved from sandstone by glaciers during the last Ice Age and boasts beautiful rock formations. It is home to strange balls of light, and ghosts, but the most interesting are the legends of gnomes and trolls.

According to legend, shy but vengeful trolls live in hiding in the Punch Bowl. Visitors who joke about the trolls often walk back to their vehicle to find it won't start. However, those who leave Skittles for the trolls have no problem starting their vehicles and heading home.

There's been only one sighting of a gnome, and it's un-confirmed at that; it tells of a little man with a white beard and pointed hat who scampered up the side of a rock and disappeared into a tunnel.

Although eyewitnesses to these creatures are scarce, trolls and gnomes are worth a mention.

Hodag

In the 1890s, folks around the town of Rhinelander began talking about a beast the size of a bear with the head and face of a grinning frog, stumpy legs, and the tail of a stegosaurus.

The monster was first reported by Eugene Shepard, a local surveyor who liked to pull pranks. He organized a party armed with dynamite and hunted the beast, which apparently only ate white bulldogs. He claimed they killed it, producing a picture of scorched remains.

A few years after, Shepard said he'd captured a Hodag using bear wrestlers and chloroform. He then displayed it at county fairs throughout Wisconsin. As attention toward the Hodag grew nationally, Shepard admitted the animal was a hoax.

Bigfoot

With 46 percent of the state covered in forestland, Wisconsin is a perfect home for Bigfoot. Here's one encounter from the *Milwaukee Journal-Sentinel*.

James Hughes, a newspaper delivery driver in Clark County, encountered an eight-foot-tall humanlike creature covered in dark gray hair. The monster stepped across the road in front of Hughes. Oddly, it was carrying a goat.

"It was walking on two legs, and it was mighty, mighty big," Hughes told the *Journal-Sentinel.* "You better believe I was scared."

But he still got a good look at the goat-carrying creature. It weighed at least five hundred pounds, had an apelike face, and had honey-colored spots on its fur. One look was all he needed. Hughes sped away from the scene and reported his sighting to the Clark County Sheriff's Department.

CHAPTER 50
WYOMING

ALTHOUGH WYOMING IS ONE of the largest of the fifty states, it has the smallest population—only 586,107 as of 2015. The city of Milwaukee, Wisconsin, alone has more people than Wyoming. The geography of Wyoming is stunning, with two-thirds of the state made up of the Rocky Mountains, the rest being the High Plains. Yellowstone and Grand Teton National Parks are in Wyoming, as is Devils Tower (of *Close Encounters of the Third Kind* fame). Nearly ten million acres of the state are covered in forest.

Farming is a big part of what makes Wyoming thrive, as are the coal, natural gas, and oil industries. Famous residents of Wyoming include Buffalo Bill Cody, sportscaster Curt Gowdy, and Han Solo himself, Harrison Ford (born in Chicago, lives in Wyoming). The state is also known for a mummy named Pedro.

JACKALOPE

San Pedro Mountains Mummy

Prospectors Cecil Mayne and Frank Carr were blasting for gold in the San Pedro Mountains in October 1932 when their dynamite uncovered a room inside the stone that was only about four feet tall, according to the Wyoming State Historical Society. The room wasn't the strange part. The strange part was what was in the room. The prospectors had found a mummified fully-grown human sitting with its legs crossed. The mummy was only a foot tall and had the face of an old man. This find gave rise to talk about the Shoshone Indian tribe's stories of small, violent humans called Nimerigar who would attack the Shoshone with small bows that shot poison-tipped arrows.

Scientists at the University of Wyoming X-rayed the mummy and claimed it was a small, misshapen child that had been killed by a blow to the head. Other reports claimed it was a fully-grown adult who died when he was in his sixties. Whatever, or whoever, it was, Pedro was displayed in a Meeteetse drug store until the figure was sold to a businessman from Casper. In the 1950s it was sold to New Yorker Leonard Wadler and has since disappeared. Whether it is the mummy of a Nimerigar, or the sad case of a deformed child, it remains a legendary piece of Wyoming history.

DeSmet Lake Monster

The dark blue waters of Lake DeSmet stretch over 258 acres under the shadow of the Bighorn Mountains in Johnson County, Wyoming. This popular fishing destination boasts not only rainbow trout, but also legends.

The local Crow Indians claimed the waters of the lake had the ability to heal and to cause visions. One of those visions poisoned the mind of a young warrior who fell in love with a water spirit and spurned the woman who was to soon become his wife. In her sadness, the woman drowned herself, and her father killed the warrior who had driven her to suicide. When the wind moans across the surface of DeSmet Lake, it is supposedly carried by the dead warrior.

The first white man to see the lake was Jesuit missionary Father Pierre DeSmet in the 1840s. By this time the local Native Americans had become fearful of the lake—not only because of the tragic legend of the dead lovers, but because of what people would later call Smetty.

When white settlers came to the area, some reported seeing a serpent swimming in the lake. It was as big around as a tree and about forty feet long. It had a head like a horse and a bony ridge down its back. Stories from the tribes near the lake claim the monster had been known to snatch people from the banks and disappear with them into the depths that are allegedly lined with bottomless tunnels.

Railroad surveyor Edward Gillette highlighted the experience the Barkey family had with Smetty in his 1925 book *Locating the Iron Trail*: "They had seen two sea serpents which had made a great commotion in the water, and swam as fast as a horse could trot. Mrs. Barkey stated that 'they looked like a long telephone pole with lard buckets attached,' referring no doubt to the fins or flappers along their sides."

Bigfoot

A story about monsters in a sparsely populated, mountainous state wouldn't be complete without a Bigfoot story. This one occurred in Yellowstone National Park, per *National Geographic*. A video by Mary Greeley shows what may, or may not, be four Bigfoot moving out of the trees and observing a herd of American bison.

Real? Fake? Michel Sartori, a zoologist at the Museum of Zoology in Lausanne, Switzerland, told *National Geographic* it was a fake. "I had two looks at the video, and although I am not a specialist in digital images, the fake is obvious in my opinion. The four of them are visible at the beginning, but for an obscure reason three of them disappeared behind a quite small fir tree … and the one who walks has quite a mechanical way of moving. All this makes this video quite suspect at best."

Regardless, this disputed Bigfoot sighting doesn't account for the numerous reports of the big hairy fellow across the state each year.

Jackalope

John Colter had already secured his place in history as a member of the Lewis and Clark Expedition (1804–1806), the first expedition to cross western North America. Then he became the first white man to see the Teton Mountain Range and enter what would in 1872 become Yellowstone National Park. But Colter didn't stop there. He claimed to see a jackalope.

The legendary jackalope is a large rabbit with antlers that can run ninety miles per hour and use human words. This creature has been reported not only in Wyoming, but throughout the American West. It has a German cousin, the wolpertinger, which has antlers, bird wings, and fangs. Dismissed as fanciful, Colter's jackalope report was soon forgotten.

For jackalope enthusiasts, the legend of the creature began in 1939 in Douglas, Wyoming, when taxidermist Douglas Herrick and his brother Ralph began selling mounted rabbit heads with antlers they'd attached, and everyone seemed to want one. Ten years later the town dubbed itself the Jackalope Capital of the World.

More than once the Wyoming state legislature has considered a bill to make the jackalope the official state mythical creature. For some reason these bills keep failing.

Jackalopes aren't real—unless, of course, they are. Two different strains of the papillomatosis virus are known to attack rabbits, raising horn-like tumors on the top of their head. Papillomatosis is also called "Jackalopism."

So, what did Colter—and others after him—see? A diseased rabbit, or something much more cryptic?

Conclusion

ARE THERE MONSTERS? AND I mean real monsters?

Some of the reports in this book are fantastic; Pennsylvania's Squonk, Colorado's Slide Rock Bolter, and Washington State's Batsquatch are among them. But the answer to the question "are there monsters?" isn't my call. I've never seen a monster, but thousands of people worldwide do every year. I'm siding with them.

This is one of the problems with proving the existence of monsters. Eyewitness accounts of a crime put people in jail; eyewitness accounts of monsters put people under ridicule. But the evidence is out there. Lots of it. Let's look at evidence for one of the most famous monsters of all—Nessie.

The first Loch Ness Monster sighting was in 565 CE by Irish monk Saint Columba. He confronted a giant beast dragging a fisherman into the water in the River Ness. Since then more than a thousand people have seen the creature. One thousand. Sure, the most famous evidence, the 1933 Surgeon's photo (showing a plesiosaur-like neck sticking above the surface of the loch) is a fake, but that doesn't diminish the thousand other witness accounts.

One thousand witnesses, however, is nothing.

There have been more than three thousand Sasquatch sightings in the United States alone since the 1920s. That means more than three thousand people have witnessed a Bigfoot in their yard, or walking across a road in front of their car, or glaring at them in the forest by the light of a campfire. There are also people like Canadian prospector Albert Ostman who have had direct encounters with one of these enormous, apish monsters. Ostman claimed that while he camped in the forest in 1924, a Sasquatch picked him up in his sleeping bag, flopped him over a shoulder, and ran off with him. The creature took Ostman to an encampment of Bigfoot and held him for six days until the prospector fed the male snuff and escaped during the beast's negative reaction. Authorities who questioned Ostman were convinced he told the truth.

Did this really happen? I don't know. Did the Pascagoula River Alien sighting really happen? Maybe. Did rancher Israel Ammon Hutchins's encounter with the Shunka Warak'in really happen? Well, yes, because Hutchins shot the monster and there's a body, mounted and put on display.

So, the answer is, yeah, you betcha. Monsters are real. I mentioned there were more than three thousand Bigfoot reports in the United States. That's important because this is just from the US. As you've read, the Pacific Northwest doesn't have a singular claim to Bigfoot, and neither does North America. There are Bigfoot stories from every continent except Antarctica. There's even an Australian Bigfoot, and along with Australian tradition, it has a great name—the Yowie. There are stories of dragons, vampires, were-creatures, giant lizards, and enormous birds from across the globe as well. These stories span continents and centuries. How do reportedly unconnected civilizations have the same monster stories?

Science has tried to explain this. According to *Smithsonian* magazine, Chinese historian Chang Qu uncovered a dinosaur fossil in the Sichuan Province in the fourth century BCE Maybe, just maybe this happened all over the world. Really? Another explanation comes from our own brains. Anthropologist David E. Jones postulates in his book *An Instinct for Dragons* that all cultures have the dragon legend simply out of instinct. Humans are wired to be afraid of large animals such as lizards, birds, and cats. Combine these animals and we get the general worldwide description of a dragon.

Uh, okay.

Given the amount of evidence for these monsters—the eyewitness accounts, the footprints, the property damage, and the DNA samples—if the case wasn't about trying to prove the existence of monsters, one would probably be recognized by a court of law.

That's my claim and I'm sticking with it. So camp, go out for a late-night country drive, and take a walk on a dark, lonely lane—you never know what you're going to run into.

BIBLIOGRAPHY

Alabama

The White Thang, *Legends and Lore of Birmingham and Central Alabama,* by Beverly Crider, 2014.

The Wampus Cat, *Mobile Press-Register,* May 30, 2015; *McDowell News,* July 29, 2009.

The Alabama Metal Man, "1973: The Alabama Tinfoil Alien," by B J Booth, 2002, NICAP.

Alaska

Living Mammoths, *The Portland (Maine) Press,* November 28, 1896.

Iliamna Lake Monster, KDLG, 670AM/89.9FM, June 19, 2017.

Kodiak Dinosaur, *Kodiak Mirror,* April 15, 1969.

Giant birds, *Anchorage Daily News*, October 18, 2002.

Steller's Sea Ape, *De Bestiis Marinis (The Beasts of the Sea),* by Georg Wilhelm Steller, 1751.

Were-otter, *Alpinist Magazine,* June 15, 2015. TMZ, August 28, 2013.

Arizona

Mogollon Monster, *The Arizona Republican,* June 3, 1903.

Dragons, *Mysteries and Miracles of Arizona,* by Jack Kutz, 1992; *Tombstone Epitaph,* April 26, 1890.

Werewolves, personal interview with Earl.

Giants, *The Complete Guide to Mysterious Beings,* by John Keel, 1994.

Arkansas

Fouke Monster, *Texarkana Gazette,* May 2, 1971/June 3, 2017.

Ozark Howler, Fayetteville and Fort Smith's 40/29 News, December 15, 2015.

Gowrow, *Arkansas Gazette,* January 31, 1897

Hyenas, arkansashunting.net, August 13, 2011.

White River Monster, *Christian County Headliner News,* April 12, 2017.

Pterosaur, *Christian County Headliner News,* December 13, 2014.

California

Patty, Canadian Broadcasting Corporation, October 26, 2017.

Dark Watchers, "Such Counsels You Gave to Me," by Robinson Jeffers, 1937; "Flight," by John Steinbeck, 1938.

The **Billiwhack Monster,** *Ghosts of Ventura County's Heritage Valley,* by Evie Ybarra, 2016.

The **Black Demon,** Discovery News, 2008.

Evil Gnomes, personal interview with Tammy.

Giant Cockroaches, personal interview with Peggy.

Colorado

Living Dinosaurs, *Empire Magazine,* August 22, 1982.

Slide Rock Bolter, *Fearsome Creatures of the Lumberwoods,* by William T. Cox, 1910.

Vampires, *The Denver Post,* June 29, 2010.

Connecticut

The **Black Dog of Hanging Hills,** *Connecticut Quarterly,* April-June 1898.

Melon Heads, *Torrington Register-Citizen,* May 23, 2010.

Sea Monsters, *The New York Times,* July 3, 1881; *Chicago Tribune,* July 17, 1895.

Glastonbury Glawackus, *The Hartford Courant,* August 21, 2014.

Delaware

Selbyville Swamp Monster, http://www.coastalpoint.com /content/swamp_story.

Mhuwe, native-languages.org.

Zwaanendael Merman, *Wilmington News Journal,* June 14, 2015.

Bigfoot, Bigfoot Field Research Organization, January 2004, August 2010, November 2012.

Florida

Myakka Skunk Ape, *Smithsonian Magazine,* March 6, 2014.

Lake Clinch Monster, *A History of Polk County,* by M.F. Hetherington, 1928; *My Pioneer Days in Florida, 1876-1898,* by Emily Bell, 1928.

Muck Monster, lagoonkeepers.org.

Sauropod Dinosaur, *Weird Florida: Your Travel Guide to Florida's Local Legends and Best Kept Secrets,* by Charlie Carlson, 2009.

St. Augustine Monster, Smithsonian Institution Archives, 1995.

Georgia

Altamaha-ha, *Savannah Georgian,* April 18, 1830.

Emily Burt, the Georgia Werewolf, findagrave.com.

Hogzilla, *ABC News,* March 21, 2005; *National Geographic,* March 22, 2005.

Beavershark, *Lake Destination Lanier Magazine,* July 18, 2016.

The Wog, *The Early History of Jackson County Georgia,* by G.J.N. Wilson, 1914.

Hawaii

Menehune, personal interview with Lisa.

Pterodactyl, cases not specific enough for a reference.

Mu, cases not specific enough for a reference.

Mo'o, cases not specific enough for a reference.

Idaho

Bear Lake Monster, *Deseret News,* August 5, 1868.

Sharlie, KTVB Channel 7, July 3, 2016.

Living Dinosaur, *Carbon County News,* December 17, 1909.

Illinois

The Enfield Monster, WWKI, April 25, 1973.

Farm City Monster, *Bloomington Pantagraph,* July 17, 1970.

Cole Hollow Road Monster, cases not specific enough for a reference.

Flying humanoids, *Chicago Tribune,* July 29, 2017.

Tuttle Bottoms Monster, *The Harrisburg Daily Register,* November 2, 2010.

Murphysboro Mud Monster, *The Southern Illinoisan,* October 26, 2005.

Indiana

The Green Clawed Beast, WKDQ, August 21, 1955.

Mill Race Monster, *The Columbus Republic,* November 2, 1974.

The Beast of Busco, *The Columbus Republic,* March 30, 1949.

Crawfordsville Monster, *Crawfordsville Journal,* September 5, 1891.

Monster Snakes, *Lafayette Courier,* September 3, 1889.

Meshekenabek, *Recollections of the Early Settlements of the Wabash Valley,* by Sandford C. Cox, 1859; *Logansport Telegraph,* July 21, 1838.

Crosley Monster, *North Vernon Plain Dealer Sun,* October 24, 2011; *Brown County Democrat,* February 23, 2016.

Iowa

Van Meter Monster, *Des Moines Register,* July 1, 2015; *Des Moines Daily News*, October 3, 1903.

Lockridge Monster, *Milwaukee Sentinel,* October 28, 1975.

Hairy Wildwoman, *The Dubuque Herald,* July 17, 1884.

Monster Turtle of Big Blue, *Mason City Globe Gazette,* October 30, 2005.

Kansas

Dogman, cases not specific enough for a reference.

Pterosaur, livepterosaur.com.

Bigfoot, Gulf Coast Bigfoot Research Organization, September 14, 2012.

Zombies, Kansas Division of Emergency Management, 2014.

Kentucky

The Pope Lick Monster, cases not specific enough for a reference.

Herrington Lake Monster, *The Courier-Journal,* August 7, 1972; *Central Kentucky News,* September 12, 2005.

Devil Monkeys, cases not specific enough for a reference.

Milton Lizard, *A Menagerie of Mysterious Beasts: Encounters with Cryptid Creatures,* by Ken Gerhard, 2016.

The Kentucky Mothman, cases not specific enough for a reference.

The Demon Leaper, Wave 3 News, 2014; *New York Times,* September 12, 1880.

Hopkinsville Goblins, *Evansville Courier and Press,*
　　August 21, 2017.

Louisiana

The Rougaru, cases not specific enough for a reference.

The Grunch, cases not specific enough for a reference.

Sea Monster, *Gulf Coast Historical Review,* Fall 1991.

Honey Island Swamp Monster, *Country Roads Magazine,*
　　September 22, 2015.

Maine

Cassie, *The Bangor Daily News,* June 5, 2017.

Pocomoonshine Lake Monster, cases not specific enough for a
　　reference.

The White Monkey, etravelmaine.com.

Specter Moose, cases not specific enough for a reference.

Bigfoot, *The Bangor Daily News,* June 22, 2015.

Wendigo, cases not specific enough for a reference.

Maryland

Snallygaster, *The Baltimore Sun,* October 24, 2013.

The Goatman, *Modern Farmer,* September 16, 2013;
　　Washington Post, November 30, 1971.

Chessie, cases not specific enough for a reference.

The Sykesville Monster, *The Carroll County Times,*
　　June 14, 1973; phantomsandmonsters.com.

Massachusetts

Pukwudgie, cases not specific enough for a reference.

Thunderbird, *The Boston Globe,* October 25, 2013; cryptozoologynews.com.

Dover Demon, *The Boston Globe,* October 29, 2006.

Beast of Truro, *The New York Times,* January 17, 1982.

Gloucester Sea Serpent, *An account of two voyages to New-England: made during the years 1638, 1663,* by John Josselyn, 1865.

Michigan

Nain Rouge, *Detroit Metro Times,* March 16, 2016.

Mishipeshu, cases not specific enough for a reference.

Michigan Mermen, cases not specific enough for a reference.

The Dogman, *The Huffington Post,* October 26, 2012.

Sea Monsters, *The Grand Rapids Press,* June 25, 1976.

Dewey Lake Monster, WWMT Newschannel 3, May 30, 2016.

Minnesota

Minnesota Iceman, *Scientific American,* January 8, 2017.

The Mystery Monster, *The Minneapolis Star-Tribune,* August 6, 2011.

Pepie, *The Star-Tribune,* July 21, 2014.

The Wendigo, cases not specific enough for a reference.

Mississippi

Mississippi Mermaid, Smithsonian Institution (www.si.edu); *New Orleans Times-Picayune,* July 24, 1892.

River Monsters, cases not specific enough for a reference.

Mississippi Mud Man, *Jackson Clarion-Ledger,* August 25, 2014.

Pascagoula River Aliens, *New York Daily News,*
October 11, 2013.

Missouri

Space Penguins, *Jefferson City News Tribune,* February 1967.

Momo, Missouri Folklore Society; *St. Louis Riverfront Times,*
October 31, 2012.

Serpent of Mud Lake, *Hawarden Independent,*
September 19, 1895.

The Piasa, *Hidden Animals: A Field Guide to Batsquatch, Chupacabra,
and Other Elusive Creatures,* by Michael Newton, 2009.

Giants, *The New York Times,* April 9, 1885.

The Night People, personal interview with Vern Windsor.

Montana

Shunka Warak'in, *Bozeman Daily Chronicle,* November 14,
2007; *Trails to Nature's Mysteries: The Life of a Working
Naturalist,* by Ross Hutchins, 1977.

A Hairy, Bear-Eating Monster, *Brooklyn Eagle,* November 4,
1892.

The Flathead Lake Monster, KECI, July 6, 2012.

Thunderbirds, https://www.thecryptocrew.com/2014/04/.

Nebraska

Alkali Lake Monster, Nebraska State Historical Society.

The Loess Man, *Science Magazine,* November 16, 1906; *Skeletal remains suggesting or attributed to early man in North America,* by Ales Hrdlicka, 1907.

Phantom Kangaroos, The Associated Press, July 28, 1958.

Vampire, Nebraska State Historical Society, https://history .nebraska.gov/blog/vampires-nebraska.

Bigfoot, *Omaha World Herald,* September 8, 2013.

Nevada

Tahoe Tessie, *Los Angeles Times,* May 3, 2005.

Jarbidge Monster, cases not specific enough for a reference.

Pterosaur, http://cryptozoologynews.com/two-people-spot -dinosaur-bird-in-nevada/.

Lovelock Skull, cases not specific enough for a reference.

Gargantuan Gliders, *Flying Saucers Magazine,* October 1959.

New Hampshire

Devil Monkeys, cases not specific enough for a reference.

Wood Devils, cases not specific enough for a reference.

Dublin Lake Monster, *America's Loch Ness Monsters,* by Philip Rife, 2000.

Pukwudgie, cases not specific enough for a reference.

New Jersey

The Jersey Devil, cases not specific enough for a reference.

Wemategunis, cases not specific enough for a reference.

Big Red Eye, CBS2, August 4, 2011.

The White Stag, cases not specific enough for a reference.

New Mexico

Weird Legends of Bottomless Lakes, Roswell, New Mexico, *Centennial Magazine,* September 2012.

Giants, *New York Times,* February 11, 1902.

Teratorns, KRQE News, July 28, 2007.

Spring-Heeled Jack, cases not specific enough for a reference.

New York

Wildmen, *Voices: The Journal of New York Folklore,* Fall-Winter 2009.

Cardiff Giant, https://www.history.com/news/the-cardiff -giant-fools-the-nation-145-years-ago.

East River Monster, *New York Daily News,* July 25, 2012.

Champ, *The Plattsburgh Republican,* July 24, 1819.

Old Greeny, *The Ithaca Journal,* January 5, 1897.

Seneca Lake Monster, *Seneca Daily News,* October 30, 2012.

Kipsy, cases not specific enough for a reference.

North Carolina

Normie, www.lakenormanmonster.com.

The Beast of Bladenboro, cases not specific enough for a reference.

Demon Dog of Valle Crucis, cases not specific enough for a reference.

The Moon-Eyed People, cases not specific enough for a reference.

North Dakota

Devils Lake Monster, *Grand Forks Daily Herald,* July 21, 1915.

The Miniwashitu, North Dakota State Historical Society.

Bigfoot, *Aberdeen American News,* March 3, 2004; *Stevens Point Journal,* January 14, 1913.

Thunderbird, cases not specific enough for a reference.

Ohio

Ohio Grassman, *Altered Dimensions* magazine, April 14, 2015.

Mill Lake Monster, *Richland Source,* October 29, 2015; *Curious Encounters: Phantom Trains, Spooky Spots and Other Mysterious Wonders,* by Loren Coleman, 1989.

Orange Eyes, cases not specific enough for a reference.

The Loveland Frogs, cases not specific enough for a reference.

Bessie, cases not specific enough for a reference.

Mothman, cases not specific enough for a reference.

Oklahoma

Oklahoma Octopus, *Scientific American Magazine,* December 19, 2013.

El Reno Chicken Man, The Associated Press, December 1970.

Elkman, personal interview with Nick.

Boar Man, cases not specific enough for a reference.

Lawton Wolf Man, cases not specific enough for a reference.

Oregon

Wally, cases not specific enough for a reference.

Colossal Claude, cases not specific enough for a reference.

Bigfoot, *The Oregonian,* November 12, 2015.

Dogman, cases not specific enough for a reference.

Cadborosaurus, cases not specific enough for a reference.

Pennsylvania

The Squonk, *Fearsome Creatures of the Lumberwoods,* by William T. Cox, 1910.

Werewolves, http://www.dogmanresearch.com/2013/04 /pennsylvania-sightings.html.

Raystown Ray, cases not specific enough for a reference.

Tommyknockers, cases not specific enough for a reference.

Albatwitch, cases not specific enough for a reference.

The Butler Gargoyle, http://www.stangordon.info /wp/2012/08/13/has-the-winged-humanoid -returned-to-butler-county-pennsylvania-9/.

Rhode Island

Bigfoot, *Coventry Patch,* October 26, 2011.

The Block Ness Monster, The Associated Press, September 6, 1996.

Sea Monster of Teddy's Beach, WPRI 12 Eyewitness News, 2007.

A Vampire, case not specific enough for a reference.

South Carolina

Lizard Man, *Charleston Post and Courier,* August 9, 2017.

Third Eye Man, *The Daily Gamecock,* October 27, 2016.

Boo Hag, case not specific enough for a reference.

Messie, The Lake Murray Monster, *Weird Carolinas,* by Roger Manly, 2011.

The Pink Mess of Goose Creek Lagoon, *St. Petersburg (Florida) Times,* December 7, 1948.

Bigfoot, *Free Times,* February 19, 2014.

South Dakota

Living Dinosaurs, case not specific enough for a reference.

Taku-He, case not specific enough for a reference.

The Little Devils of Spirit Mound, explorer William Clark's journal; explorer Sergeant John Ordway's journal.

Banshee of the Badlands, case not specific enough for a reference.

Lake Kampeska Monster, *Watertown Public Opinion,* July 19, 2008; *South Dakota Magazine* January/February 2007 issue.

Two-Faced Monster, case not specific enough for a reference.

Tennessee

Tennessee Wildman, *The Hagerstown Mail,* May 5, 1871.

The Flintville Monster, *The Augusta Georgia Chronicle,* April 6, 1997

White Screamer, case not specific enough for a reference.

The Tennessee Terror, case not specific enough for a reference.

Hairy Human on Four Legs, case not specific enough for a reference.

Texas

The Lake Worth Monster, NBCDFW-5, August 8, 2009.

La Lechuza, case not specific enough for a reference.

Black-Eyed Kids, personal interview with Brian Bethel.

Big Bird, *San Antonio Current,* January 20, 2012; *The Brownsville Herald,* November 7, 2004.

Pterodactyl, *The Truth About Dinosaurs: The Witness of Creation Series Volume Five,* by Billy Crone, 2017.

Mountain Boomer, *Mountain Boomer,* by Jimmy Ward, 1993.

Chupacabra, case not specific enough for a reference.

Bigfoot, case not specific enough for a reference.

Utah

Flying reptiles, *Ogden Standard-Examiner,* July 23, 1894.

Bear Lake Monster, *Deseret News,* July 27, 1868; Deseret News, July 12, 2004.

Great Salt Lake Whales, *Utah Enquirer,* June 24, 1890; Deseret News, October 3, 1995.

Giants, *New York Sun,* August 27, 1891.

Bigfoot, *Standard-Examiner,* August 25, 1977.

Vermont

Northfield Pigman, *Quail Bell Magazine,* December 2, 2013.

The Awful, *County Courier,* October 6, 2006.

Memphre, *The Stanstead Journal,* January 21, 1847; *Huffington Post,* October 15, 2012.

Willy, *Willoughby Caledonian,* August 14, 1868; The International Dracontology Society of Lake Memphrémagog, http://www.memphre.com/ang.html.

Champ, *Plattsburgh Republican,* July 24, 1819.

Bigfoot, NBC5, Nov. 29, 2012; April 12, 2012.

Virginia

Bunny Man, *The Washington Post,* October 22, 1970.

Giant Birds, case not specific enough for a reference.

Werewolf, InsideNoVa.com, October 24, 2011.

Snallygaster, case not specific enough for a reference.

Bigfoot, WTVR, July 2, 2014.

Washington

Batsquatch, *The Tacoma News Tribune,* April 19, 1994.

Cadborosaurus, *Global News,* August 29, 2011.

Basket Ogress, case not specific enough for a reference.

Drunken Bears, *NBC News,* August 19, 2004.

A Whole Bunch of Bigfoot, *The Philadelphia Inquirer,* January 16, 2014; *Bremerton Sun,* July 10, 2000.

Rock Lake Monster, *The Spokesman-Review,* April 9, 1995.

West Virginia

Mothman, *Point Pleasant Register,* November 16, 1966; WCHS-TV, November 22, 2016.

Sheepsquatch, *Modern Farmer Magazine,* December 12, 2013.

Flatwoods Monster, case not specific enough for a reference.

Ogua, case not specific enough for a reference.

Appalachian Black Panther, *The Naturalist's Library, Mammalia, Vol. 1, Cats,* by Sir William Jardine, 1843.

Stone Man, case not specific enough for a reference.

Wisconsin

Werewolves, *The Beast of Bray Road: Tailing Wisconsin's Werewolf,* by Linda S. Godfrey, 2003.

Lake Koshkonong Monster, *Watertown Republican,* November 1887.

Jenny, *Lake and Sea Monsters,* by Linda S. Godfrey, 2008.

Goatman of Hogsback Road, case not specific enough for a reference.

Mineral Point Vampire, case not specific enough for a reference.

Trolls and gnomes, case not specific enough for a reference.

Hodag, Wisconsin Historical Society, https://www.wisconsin history.org/Records/Article/CS1628.

Bigfoot, *Milwaukee Journal-Sentinel,* April 4, 2000.

Wyoming

San Pedro Mountains Mummy, Wyoming State Historical Society, https://www.wyohistory.org/encyclopedia /pedro-mountain-mummy.

DeSmet Lake Monster, *Locating the Iron Trail,* by Edward Gillette, 1925.

Bigfoot, *National Geographic,* February 15, 2015.

Jackalope, case not specific enough for a reference.

Index

To Write the Author

If you wish to contact the author or would like more information about this book, please write to the author in care of Llewellyn Worldwide, and we will forward your request. Both the author and publisher appreciate hearing from you and learning of your enjoyment of this book and how it has helped you. Llewellyn Worldwide cannot guarantee that every letter written to the author can be answered, but all will be forwarded. Please write to:

Jason Offutt
℅ Llewellyn Worldwide
2143 Wooddale Drive
Woodbury, MN 55125-2989

Please enclose a self-addressed stamped envelope for reply,
or $1.00 to cover costs. If outside the U.S.A., enclose
an international postal reply coupon.